ISBN 978-1-4400-6687-0
PIBN 10081161

1 MONTH OF
FREE
READING

at

www.ForgottenBooks.com

English
Français
Deutsche
Italiano
Español
Português

www.forgottenbooks.com

Mythology Photography **Fiction**
Fishing Christianity **Art** Cooking
Essays Buddhism Freemasonry
Medicine **Biology** Music **Ancient**
Egypt Evolution Carpentry Physics
Dance Geology **Mathematics** Fitness
Shakespeare **Folklore** Yoga Marketing
Confidence Immortality Biographies
Poetry **Psychology** Witchcraft
Electronics Chemistry History **Law**
Accounting **Philosophy** Anthropology
Alchemy Drama Quantum Mechanics
Atheism Sexual Health **Ancient History**
Entrepreneurship Languages Sport
Paleontology Needlework Islam
Metaphysics Investment Archaeology
Parenting Statistics Criminology
Motivational

MEDEA

EURIPIDES

THE MEDEA

TRANSLATED INTO ENGLISH RHYMING VERSE

WITH EXPLANATORY NOTES BY

GILBERT MURRAY

O.M.

FORMERLY REGIUS PROFESSOR OF GREEK IN THE
UNIVERSITY OF OXFORD

LONDON
GEORGE ALLEN & UNWIN LTD
MUSEUM STREET

FIRST PUBLISHED FEBRUARY 1910
REPRINTED MARCH 1912, MARCH 1913
NOVEMBER 1919, APRIL 1921
JANUARY 1923, JULY 1927
1931, 1933, 1941, 1946, 1950
1956, 1960 AND 1965

PRINTED IN GREAT BRITAIN
in 11 *on* 12 *point Caslon Old Face*
BY UNWIN BROTHERS LIMITED
WOKING AND LONDON

INTRODUCTION

THE *Medea*, in spite of its background of wonder and enchantment, is not a romantic play but a tragedy of character and situation. It deals, so to speak, not with the romance itself, but with the end of the romance, a thing which is so terribly often the reverse of romantic. For all but the very highest of romances are apt to have just one flaw somewhere, and in the story of Jason and Medea the flaw was of a fatal kind.

The wildness and beauty of the Argo legend run through all Greek literature, from the mass of Corinthian lays older than our present Iliad, which later writers vaguely associate with the name of Eumêlus, to the Fourth Pythian Ode of Pindar and the beautiful Argonautica of Apollonius Rhodius. Our poet knows the wildness and the beauty; but it is not these qualities that he specially seeks. He takes them almost for granted, and pierces through them to the sheer tragedy that lies below.

Jason, son of Aeson, King of Iôlcos, in Thessaly, began his life in exile. His uncle Pelias had seized his father's kingdom, and Jason was borne away to the mountains by night and given, wrapped in a purple robe, to Chiron, the Centaur. When he reached manhood he came down to Iôlcos to demand, as Pindar tells us, his ancestral honour, and stood in the market-place, a world-famous figure, onesandalled, with his pard-skin, his two spears and his long hair, gentle and wild and fearless, as the Wise Beast had reared him. Pelias, cowed but loath to yield, promised to give up the kingdom if Jason would make his way to the unknown land of Colchis and perform a double quest. First, if I read Pindar aright, he must fetch back the soul of his kinsman Phrixus, who had died there far from home; and, secondly, find the fleece of the Golden Ram which Phrixus had sacrificed. Jason undertook the quest: gathered the most daring heroes from all parts of Hellas; built the first ship, Argo, and set to sea. After all manner of desperate adventures he reached the land of Aiêtês, king of the Colchians, and there hope failed him. By policy, by tact, by sheer courage he did all that man could do. But Aiêtês was both hostile and treacherous. The Argonauts were surrounded, and their destruction seemed only a question of days when, suddenly, unasked, and by the mercy of Heaven, Aiêtês' daughter, Mêdêa, an enchantress as well as a princess, fell in love with Jason. She helped him through all his trials; slew for him her own sleepless serpent, who guarded the fleece; deceived her father, and secured both the fleece and the soul of Phrixus. At the last moment it appeared that her brother, Absyrtus, was about to lay an ambush for Jason. She invited Absyrtus to her room, stabbed him dead, and fled with Jason over the seas. She had given up all, and expected in return a perfect love.

And what of Jason? He could not possibly avoid taking Medea with him. He probably rather loved her. She formed at the least a brilliant addition to the glory of his enterprise. Not many heroes could produce a barbarian princess ready to leave all and follow them in blind trust. For of course, as every one knew without the telling in fifth-century Athens, no legal marriage was possible between a Greek and a barbarian from Colchis.

All through the voyage home, a world-wide baffled voyage by the Ister and the Eridanus and the African Syrtes, Medea was still in her element, and proved a constant help and counsellor to the Argonauts. When they reached Jason's home, where Pelias was still king, things began to be different. An ordered and law-abiding Greek state was scarcely the place for the untamed Colchian. We only know the catastrophe. She saw with smothered rage how Pelias hated Jason and was bent on keeping the kingdom from him, and she determined to do her lover another act of splendid service. Making the most of her fame as an enchantress, she persuaded Pelias that he could, by a certain process, regain his youth. He eagerly caught at the hope. His daughters tried the process upon him, and Pelias died in agony. Surely Jason would be grateful now!

The real result was what it was sure to be in a civilised country. Medea and her lover had to fly for their lives, and Jason was debarred for ever from succeeding to the throne of Iôlcos. Probably there was another result also in Jason's mind: the conclusion that at all costs he must somehow separate himself from this wild beast of a woman who was ruining his life. He directed their flight to Corinth, governed at the time by a ruler of some sort, whether " tyrant " or king, who was growing old and had an only daughter. Creon would naturally want a son-in-law to support and succeed him. And where in all Greece could he find one stronger or more famous than the chief of the Argonauts? If only Medea were not there! No doubt Jason owed her a great debt for her various services. Still, after all, he was not married to her. And a man must not be weak in such matters as these. Jason accepted the princess's hand, and when Medea became violent, found it difficult to be really angry with Creon for instantly condemning her to exile. At this point the tragedy begins.

[The *Medea* is one of the earliest of Euripides' works now preserved to us. And those of us who have in our time glowed at all with the religion of realism will probably feel in it many of the qualities of youth. Not, of course, the more normal, sensuous, romantic youth, the youth of *Romeo and Juliet*; but another kind—crude, austere, passionate—the youth of the poet who is also a sceptic and a devotee of truth, who so hates the conventionally and falsely beautiful that he is apt to be unduly ascetic towards beauty itself.] When a writer really deficient in poetry walks in this path, the result is purely disagreeable. [It produces its best results when the writer, like Euripides or Tolstoy, is so possessed by an inward flame of poetry that it breaks out at the great moments and consumes the cramping theory that would hold it in.] (One can feel in the *Medea* that the natural and inevitable romance of the story is kept rigidly down. One word about Medea's ancient serpent, two or three references to the Clashing Rocks, one startling flash of light upon the real love of Jason's life, love for the

ship Argo, these are almost all the concessions made
to us by the merciless delineator of disaster into
whose hands we are fallen. Jason is a middle-aged
man, with much glory, indeed, and some illusions; but
a man entirely set upon building up a great career,
to whom love and all its works, though at times he has
found them convenient, are for the most part only
irrational and disturbing elements in a world which
he can otherwise mould to his will. And yet, most
cruel touch of all, one feels this man to be the real
Jason. It is not that he has fallen from his heroic
past. It is that he was really like this always. And
so with Medea. It is not only that her beauty has
begun to fade; not only that she is set in surroundings
which vaguely belittle and weaken her, making her
no more a bountiful princess, but only an ambiguous
and much criticised foreigner. Her very devotion of
love for Jason, now turned to hatred, shows itself
to have been always of that somewhat rank and ugly
sort to which such a change is natural.

For concentrated dramatic quality and sheer in-
tensity of passion few plays ever written can vie with
the *Medea*. Yet it obtained only a third prize at its
first production; and, in spite of its immense fame,
there are not many scholars who would put it among
their favourite tragedies. The comparative failure of
the first production was perhaps due chiefly to the
extreme originality of the play. The Athenians in
432 B.C. had not yet learnt to understand or tolerate
such work as this, though it is likely enough that they
fortified their unfavourable opinion by the sort of
criticisms which we still find attributed to Aristotle
and Dicæarchus.

At the present time it is certainly not the newness of the subject: I do not think it is Aegeus, nor yet the dragon chariot, much less Medea's involuntary burst of tears in the second scene with Jason, that really produces the feeling of dissatisfaction with which many people must rise from this great play. It is rather the general scheme on which the drama is built. It is a scheme which occurs again and again in Euripides, a study of oppression and revenge. Such a subject in the hands of a more ordinary writer would probably take the form of a triumph of oppressed virtue. But Euripides gives us nothing so sympathetic, nothing so cheap and unreal. If oppression usually made people virtuous, the problems of the world would be very different from what they are. Euripides seems at times to hate the revenge of the oppressed almost as much as the original cruelty of the oppressor; or, to put the same fact in a different light, he seems deliberately to dwell upon the twofold evil of cruelty, that it not only causes pain to the victim, but actually by means of the pain makes him a worse man, so that when his turn of triumph comes, it is no longer a triumph of justice or a thing to make men rejoice. This is a grim lesson; taught often enough by history, though seldom by the fables of the poets.

Seventeen years later than the *Medea* Euripides expressed this sentiment in a more positive way in the *Trojan Women*, where a depth of wrong borne without revenge becomes, or seems for the moment to become, a thing beautiful and glorious. But more plays are constructed like the *Medea*. The *Hecuba* begins with a noble and injured Queen, and ends with her hideous vengeance on her enemy and his innocent sons. In the *Orestes* all our hearts go out to the suffering and deserted prince, till we find at last that we have committed ourselves to the blood-thirst of a madman. In the *Electra*, the workers of the vengeance themselves repent.

The dramatic effect of this kind of tragedy is curious. No one can call it undramatic or tame. Yet it is painfully unsatisfying. At the close of the *Medea* I actually find myself longing for a *deus ex machinâ*, for some being like Artemis in the *Hippolytus* or the good Dioscuri of the *Electra*, to speak a word of explanation or forgiveness, or at least leave some sound of music in our ears to drown that dreadful and insistent clamour of hate. The truth is that in this play Medea herself is the *dea ex machinâ*. The woman whom Jason and Creon intended simply to crush has been transformed by her injuries from an individual human being into a sort of living Curse. She is inspired with superhuman force. Her wrongs and her hate fill all the sky. And the judgment pronounced on Jason comes not from any disinterested or peace-making God, but from his own victim transfigured into a devil.

From any such judgment there is an instant appeal to sane human sympathy. Jason has suffered more than enough. But that also is the way of the world. And the last word upon these tragic things is most often something not to be expressed by the sentences of even the wisest articulate judge, but only by the unspoken *lacrimæ rerum*.

G. M.

MEDEA

CHARACTERS OF THE PLAY

MEDEA, *daughter of Aiêtês, King of Colchis.*

JASON, *chief of the Argonauts; nephew of Pelias, King of Iôlcos in Thessaly.*

CREON, *ruler of Corinth.*

AEGEUS, *King of Athens.*

NURSE *of Medea.*

TWO CHILDREN *of Jason and Medea.*

ATTENDANT *on the children.*

A MESSENGER.

CHORUS of Corinthian Women, with their LEADER.
Soldiers and Attendants.

The scene is laid in Corinth. The play was first acted when Pythodôrus was Archon, Olympiad 87, year 1 (431 B.C.). Euphorion was first, Sophocles second, Euripides third, with Medea, Philoctêtes, Dictys, and the Harvesters, a Satyr-play.

MEDEA

The Scene represents the front of Medea's *House in Corinth. A road to the right leads towards the royal castle, one on the left to the harbour. The* Nurse *is discovered alone.*

Nurse.

Would God no Argo e'er had winged the seas
To Colchis through the blue Symplêgades:
No shaft of riven pine in Pêlion's glen
Shaped that first oar-blade in the hands of men
Valiant, who won, to save King Pelias' vow,
The fleece All-golden! Never then, I trow,
Mine own princess, her spirit wounded sore
With love of Jason, to the encastled shore
Had sailed of old Iôlcos: never wrought
The daughters of King Pelias, knowing not,
To spill their father's life: nor fled in fear,
Hunted for that fierce sin, to Corinth here
With Jason and her babes. This folk at need
Stood friend to her, and she in word and deed
Served alway Jason. Surely this doth bind,
Through all ill days, the hurts of humankind,
When man and woman in one music move.
But now, the world is angry, and true love

Sick as with poison.   Jason doth forsake
My mistress and his own two sons, to make
His couch in a king's chamber.   He must wed:
Wed with this Creon's child, who now is head
And chief of Corinth.   Wherefore sore betrayed
Medea calleth up the oath they made,
They two, and wakes the claspèd hands again,
The troth surpassing speech, and cries amain
On God in heaven to mark the end, and how
Jason hath paid his debt.
                         All fasting now
And cold, her body yielded up to pain,
Her days a waste of weeping, she hath lain,
Since first she knew that he was false.   Her eyes
Are lifted not; and all her visage lies
In the dust.   If friends will speak, she hears no more
Than some dead rock or wave that beats the shore:
Only the white throat in a sudden shame
May writhe, and all alone she moans the name
Of father, and land, and home, forsook that day
For this man's sake, who casteth her away.
Not to be quite shut out from home . . . alas,
She knoweth now how rare a thing that was!
Methinks she hath a dread, not joy, to see
Her children near.   'Tis this that maketh me
Most tremble, lest she do I know not what.
Her heart is no light thing, and useth not
To brook much wrong.   I know that woman, aye,
And dread her!   Will she creep alone to die
Bleeding in that old room, where still is laid
Lord Jason's bed?   She hath for that a blade
Made keen.   Or slay the bridegroom and the king,
And win herself God knows what direr thing?

'Tis a fell spirit.   Few, I ween, shall stir
Her hate unscathed, or lightly humble her.
    Ha!   'Tis the children from their games again,
Rested and gay; and all their mother's pain
Forgotten!   Young lives ever turn from gloom!
        [*The* CHILDREN *and their* ATTENDANT *come in.*

ATTENDANT.

Thou ancient treasure of my lady's room,
What mak'st thou here before the gates alone,
And alway turning on thy lips some moan
Of old mischances?   Will our mistress be
Content, this long time to be left by thee?

NURSE.

Grey guard of Jason's children, a good thrall
Hath his own grief, if any hurt befall
His   masters.   Aye,   it   holds   one's   heart!
        Meseems
I have strayed out so deep in evil dreams,
I longed to rest me here alone, and cry
Medea's wrongs to this still Earth and Sky.

ATTENDANT.

How?   Are the tears yet running in her eyes?

NURSE.

'Twere good to be like thee! .   Her sorrow lies
Scarce wakened yet, not half its perils wrought.
B

ATTENDANT.

Mad spirit! . . . if a man may speak his thought
Of masters mad.—And nothing in her ears
Hath sounded yet of her last cause for tears!

[*He moves towards the house, but the* NURSE
checks him.

NURSE.

What cause, old man? . . . Nay, grudge me not one
word.

ATTENDANT.

'Tis nothing.   Best forget what thou hast heard.

NURSE.

Nay, housemate, by thy beard!   Hold it not hid
From me. . . . I will keep silence if thou bid.

ATTENDANT.

I heard an old man talking, where he sate
At draughts in the sun, beside the fountain gate,
And never thought of me, there standing still
Beside him.   And he said, 'Twas Creon's will,
Being lord of all this land, that she be sent,
And with her her two sons, to banishment.
Maybe 'tis all false.   For myself, I know
No further, and I would it were not so.

NURSE.

Jason will never bear it—his own sons
Banished,—however hot his anger runs
Against their mother!

ATTENDANT.

Old love burneth low
When new love wakes, men say.   He is not now
Husband nor father here, nor any kin.

NURSE.

But this is ruin!   New waves breaking in
To wreck us, ere we are righted from the old!

ATTENDANT.

Well, hold thy peace.   Our mistress will be told
All in good time.   Speak thou no word hereof.

NURSE.

My babes!   What think ye of your father's love?
God curse him not, he is my master still:
But, oh, to them that loved him, 'tis an ill
Friend. . . .

ATTENDANT.

And what man on earth is different?   How?
Hast thou lived all these years, and learned but now
That every man more loveth his own head
Than other men's?   He dreameth of the bed
Of this new bride, and thinks not of his sons.

NURSE.

Go: run into the house, my little ones:
All will end happily! . . . Keep them apart:
Let not their mother meet them while her heart

Is darkened.   Yester night I saw a flame
Stand in her eyes, as though she hated them,
And would I know not what.   For sure her wrath
Will never turn nor slumber, till she hath . . .
Go: and if some must suffer, may it be
Not we who love her, but some enemy!

VOICE (*within*).

O shame and pain: O woe is me!
Would I could die in my misery!
[*The* CHILDREN *and the* ATTENDANT *go in.*

NURSE.

Ah, children, hark!   She moves again
  Her frozen heart, her sleeping wrath.
  In, quick!   And never cross her path,
Nor rouse that dark eye in its pain;

That fell sea-spirit, and the dire
  Spring of a will untaught, unbowed.
  Quick, now!—Methinks this weeping cloud
Hath in its heart some thunder-fire,

Slow gathering, that must flash ere long.
  I know not how, for ill or well,
  It turns, this uncontrollable
Tempestuous spirit, blind with wrong.

VOICE (*within*).

Have I not suffered?   Doth it call
No tears? . . . Ha, ye beside the wall
Unfathered children, God hate you
As I am hated, and him, too,
  That gat you, and this house and all!

NURSE.

For pity!   What have they to do,
   Babes, with their father's sin?   Why call
   Thy curse on these? . . . Ah, children, all
These days my bosom bleeds for you.

Rude are the wills of princes: yea,
   Prevailing alway, seldom crossed,
   On fitful winds their moods are tossed:
'Tis best men tread the equal way.

Aye, not with glory but with peace
   May the long summers find me crowned:
   For gentleness—her very sound
Is magic, and her usages

All wholesome: but the fiercely great
   Hath little music on his road,
   And falleth, when the hand of God
Shall move, most deep and desolate.
[*During the last words the* LEADER *of the Chorus
   has entered.   Other women follow her.*

LEADER.

I heard a voice and a moan,
   A voice of the eastern seas:
   Hath she found not yet her ease?
     Speak, O agèd one.
For I stood afar at the gate,
   And there came from within a cry,

And wailing desolate.
Ah, no more joy have I,
For the griefs this house doth see,
And the love it hath wrought in me.

NURSE.

There is no house! 'Tis gone.   The lord
Seeketh a prouder bed: and she
Wastes in her chamber, nor one word
Will hear of care or charity.

VOICE (*within*).

O Zeus, O Earth, O Light,
Will the fire not stab my brain?
What profiteth living?   Oh,
Shall I not lift the slow
Yoke, and let Life go,
As a beast out in the night,
To lie, and be rid of pain.

CHORUS.

Some Women.

A.

" O Zeus, O Earth, O Light: "
The cry of a bride forlorn
Heard ye, and wailing born
Of lost delight?

B.

Why weariest thou this day,
  Wild heart, for the bed abhorrèd,
The cold bed in the clay?
Death cometh though no man pray,
  Ungarlanded, un-adorèd.
      Call him not thou.

C.

If another's arms be now
  Where thine have been,
  On his head be the sin:
Rend not thy brow!

D.

All that thou sufferest,
  God seeth: Oh, not so sore
Waste nor weep for the breast
  That was thine of yore.

VOICE (*within*).

Virgin of Righteousness,
Virgin of hallowed Troth,
Ye marked me when with an oath
I bound him; mark no less
That oath's end.   Give me to see
Him and his bride, who sought
My grief when I wronged her not,
Broken in misery,

And all her house. . . . O God,
My mother's home, and the dim
Shore that I left for him,
And the voice of my brother's blood. . . .

Nurse.

Oh, wild words! Did ye hear her cry
  To them that guard man's faith forsworn,
  Themis and Zeus? . . . This wrath new-born
Shall make mad workings ere it die.

Chorus.
Other Women.

A.

Would she but come to seek
  Our faces, that love her well,
  And take to her heart the spell
    Of words that speak?

B.

Alas for the heavy hate
  And anger that burneth ever!
Would it but now abate,
Ah God, I love her yet.
  And surely my love's endeavour
    Shall fail not here.

C.

Go: from that chamber drear
    Forth to the day
Lead her, and say, Oh, say
    That we love her dear.

D.

Go, lest her hand be hard
    On the innocent: Ah, let be!
For her grief moves hitherward,
    Like an angry sea.

NURSE.

That will I: though what words of mine
    Or love shall move her?   Let them lie
    With the old lost labours! . . . Yet her eye—
Know ye the eyes of the wild kine,

The lion flash that guards their brood?
    So looks she now if any thrall
    Speak comfort, or draw near at all
My mistress in her evil mood.
                    [*The* NURSE *goes into the house.*

CHORUS.

A Woman.

Alas, the bold blithe bards of old
    That all for joy their music made,
For feasts and dancing manifold,
    That Life might listen and be glad.

But all the darkness and the wrong,
    Quick deaths and dim heart-aching things,
Would no man ease them with a song
    Or music of a thousand strings?

Then song had served us in our need.
    What profit, o'er the banquet's swell
That lingering cry that none may heed?
    The feast hath filled them: all is well!

Others.

I heard a song, but it comes no more,
    Where the tears ran over:
A keen cry but tired, tired:
A woman's cry for her heart's desired,
    For a traitor's kiss and a lost lover.
But a prayer, methinks, yet riseth sore
    To God, to Faith, God's ancient daughter—
The Faith that over sundering seas
Drew her to Hellas, and the breeze
Of midnight shivered, and the door
    Closed of the salt unsounded water.
[*During the last words* MEDEA *has come out from
    the house.*

MEDEA.

Women of Corinth, I am come to show
My face, lest ye despise me. For I know
Some heads stand high and fail not, even at night
Alone—far less like this, in all men's sight:
And we, who study not our wayfarings
But feel and cry—Oh we are drifting things,
And evil! For what truth is in men's eyes,
Which search no heart, but in a flash despise

A strange face, shuddering back from one that ne'er
Hath wronged them? . . . Sure, far-comers any-
  where,
I know, must bow them and be gentle. Nay,
A Greek himself men praise not, who alway
Should seek his own will recking not. But I—
This thing undreamed of, sudden from on high,
Hath sapped my soul: I dazzle where I stand,
The cup of all life shattered in my hand,
Longing to die—O friends! He, even he,
Whom to know well was all the world to me,
The man I loved, hath proved most evil.—Oh,
Of all things upon earth that bleed and grow,
A herb most bruised is woman. We must pay
Our store of gold, hoarded for that one day,
To buy us some man's love; and lo, they bring
A master of our flesh! There comes the sting
Of the whole shame. And then the jeopardy,
For good or ill, what shall that master be;
Reject she cannot: and if he but stays
His suit, 'tis shame on all that woman's days.
So thrown amid new laws, new places, why,
'Tis magic she must have, or prophecy—
Home never taught her that—how best to guide
Toward peace this thing that sleepeth at her side.
And she who, labouring long, shall find some way
Whereby her lord may bear with her, nor fray
His yoke too fiercely, blessed is the breath
That woman draws! Else, let her pray for death.
Her lord, if he be wearied of the face
Withindoors, gets him forth, some merrier place
Will ease his heart: but she waits on, her whole
Vision enchainèd on a single soul.

And then, forsooth, 'tis they that face the call
Of war, while we sit sheltered, hid from all
Peril!—False mocking!   Sooner would I stand
Three times to face their battles, shield in hand,
Than bear one child.

                But peace!   There cannot be
Ever the same tale told of thee and me.
Thou hast this city, and thy father's home,
And joy of friends, and hope in days to come:
But I, being citiless, am cast aside
By him that wedded me, a savage bride
Won in far seas and left—no mother near,
No brother, not one kinsman anywhere
For harbour in this storm.   Therefore of thee
I ask one thing.   If chance yet ope to me
Some path, if even now my hand can win
Strength to requite this Jason for his sin,
Betray me not!   Oh, in all things but this,
I know how full of fears a woman is,
And faint at need, and shrinking from the light
Of battle: but once spoil her of her right
In man's love, and there moves, I warn thee well,
No bloodier spirit between heaven and hell.

LEADER.

I will betray thee not.   It is but just,
Thou smite him.—And that weeping in the dust
And stormy tears, how should I blame them?
     Stay:
'Tis Creon, lord of Corinth, makes his way
Hither, and bears, methinks, some word of weight.

[Enter from the right CREON, *the King, with armed Attendants.*

CREON

Thou woman sullen-eyed and hot with hate
Against thy lord, Medea, I here command
That thou and thy two children from this land
Go forth to banishment.   Make no delay:
Seeing ourselves, the King, are come this day
To see our charge fulfilled; nor shall again
Look homeward ere we have led thy children twain
And thee beyond our realm's last boundary.

MEDEA

Lost!   Lost!
Mine haters at the helm with sail flung free
Pursuing; and for us no beach nor shore
In the endless waters! . . . Yet, though stricken sore,
I still will ask thee, for what crime, what thing
Unlawful, wilt thou cast me out, O King?

CREON.

What crime?   I fear thee, woman—little need
To cloak my reasons—lest thou work some deed
Of darkness on my child.   And in that fear
Reasons enough have part.   Thou comest here
A wise-woman confessed, and full of lore
In unknown ways of evil. Thou art sore
In heart, being parted from thy lover's arms.
And   more,   thou   hast   made   menace . . . so   the
    alarms

But now have reached mine ear . . . on bride and
    groom,
And him who gave the bride, to work thy doom
Of vengeance.   Which, ere yet it be too late,
I sweep aside.   I choose to earn thine hate
Of set will now, not palter with the mood
Of mercy, and hereafter weep in blood.

MEDEA.

'Tis not the first nor second time, O King,
That fame hath hurt me, and come nigh to bring
My ruin. . . . How can any man, whose eyes
Are wholesome, seek to rear his children wise
Beyond men's wont?   Much helplessness in arts
Of common life, and in their townsmen's hearts
Envy deep-set   . so much their learning brings!
Come unto fools with knowledge of new things,
They deem it vanity, not knowledge.   Aye,
And men that erst for wisdom were held high,
Feel thee a thorn to fret them, privily
Held higher than they.   So hath it been with me.
A wise-woman I am; and for that sin
To divers ill names men would pen me in;
A seed of strife; an eastern dreamer; one
Of brand not theirs; one hard to play upon . . .
Ah, I am not so wondrous wise!—And now,
To thee, I am terrible!   What fearest thou?
What dire deed?   Do I tread so proud a path—
Fear me not thou!—that I should brave the wrath
Of princes?   Thou: what hast thou ever done
To wrong me?   Granted thine own child to one
Whom thy soul chose.—Ah, *him* out of my heart
I hate; but thou, meseems, hast done thy part

Not ill.   And for thine houses' happiness
I hold no grudge.   Go: marry, and God bless
Your issues.   Only suffer me to rest
Somewhere within this land. Though sore oppressed,
I will be still, knowing mine own defeat.

CREON.

Thy words be gentle: but I fear me yet
Lest even now there creep some wickedness
Deep hid within thee.   And for that the less
I trust thee now than ere these words began.
A woman quick of wrath, aye, or a man,
Is easier watching than the cold and still.
    Up, straight, and find thy road!   Mock not my will
With words. This doom is passed beyond recall;
Nor all thy crafts shall help thee, being withal
My manifest foe, to linger at my side.

MEDEA (*suddenly throwing herself down and
clinging to* CREON).
Oh, by thy knees!   By that new-wedded bride

CREON.
'Tis waste of words.   Thou shalt not weaken me.

MEDEA.
Wilt hunt me?   Spurn me when I kneel to thee?

CREON.
'Tis mine own house that kneels to me, not thou.

MEDEA.

Home, my lost home, how I desire thee now!

CREON.

And I mine, and my child, beyond all things.

MEDEA.

O Loves of man, what curse is on your wings!

CREON.

Blessing or curse, 'tis as their chances flow.

MEDEA.

Remember, Zeus, the cause of all this woe!

CREON.

Oh, rid me of my pains!   Up, get the gone!

MEDEA.

What would I with thy pains?   I have mine own.

CREON.

Up: or, 'fore God, my soldiers here shall fling . . .

MEDEA.

Not that!   Not that!   I do but pray, O King

CREON.

Thou wilt not?　I must face the harsher task?

MEDEA.

I accept mine exile.　'Tis not that I ask.

CREON.

Why then so wild?　Why clinging to mine hand?

MEDEA (*rising*).

For one day only leave me in thy land
At peace, to find some counsel, ere the strain
Of exile fall, some comfort for these twain,
Mine innocents; since others take no thought,
It seems, to save the babes that they begot.
　　Ah!　Thou wilt pity them!　Thou also art
A father: thou hast somewhere still a heart
That feels. . . . I reck not of myself: 'tis they
That break me, fallen upon so dire a day.

CREON.

Mine is no tyrant's mood.　Aye, many a time
Ere this my tenderness hath marred the chime
Of wisest counsels.　And I know that now
I do mere folly.　But so be it!　Thou
Shalt have this grace　　But this I warn thee clear,
If once the morrow's sunlight find thee here
Within my borders, thee or child of thine,
Thou diest! . . . Of this judgment not a line

Shall waver nor abate.   So linger on,
If thou needs must, till the next risen sun;
No further. . . . In one day there scarce can be
Those perils wrought whose dread yet haunteth me.
[*Exit* CREON *with his suite.*

CHORUS.

O woman, woman of sorrow,
    Where wilt thou turn and flee?
What town shall be thine to-morrow,
    What land of all lands that be,
What door of a strange man's home?
    Yea, God hath hunted thee,
Medea, forth to the foam
    Of a trackless sea.

MEDEA.

Defeat on every side; what else?—But Oh,
Not here the end is: think it not!   I know
For bride and groom one battle yet untried,
And goodly pains for him that gave the bride.
    Dost dream I would have grovelled to this man,
Save that I won mine end, and shaped my plan
For merry deeds?   My lips had never deigned
Speak word with him: my flesh been never stained
With touching. . . . Fool, Oh, triple fool! It lay
So plain for him to kill my whole essay
By exile swift: and, lo, he sets me free
This one long day: wherein mine haters three
Shall lie here dead, the father and the bride
And husband—mine, not hers!   Oh, I have tried

So many thoughts of murder to my turn,
I know not which best likes me.　Shall I burn
Their house with fire?　Or stealing past unseen
To Jason's bed—I have a blade made keen
For that—stab, breast to breast, that wedded pair?
Good, but for one thing.　When I am taken there,
And killed, they will laugh loud who hate me. . .
　　　　　　　　　　　　　　　　　　　　Nay,
I love the old way best, the simple way
Of poison, where we too are strong as men.
Ah me!
And they being dead—what place shall hold me then?
What friend shall rise, with land inviolate
And trusty doors, to shelter from their hate
This flesh! . . . None anywhere!　　　A little
　　　more
I needs must wait: and, if there ope some door
Of refuge, some strong tower to shield me, good:
In craft and darkness I will hunt this blood.
Else, if mine hour be come and no hope nigh,
Then sword in hand, full-willed and sure to die,
I yet will live to slay them.　I will wend
Man-like, their road of daring to the end.
　So help me She who of all Gods hath been
The best to me, of all my chosen queen
And helpmate, Hecatê, who dwells apart,
The flame of flame, in my fire's inmost heart:
For all their strength, they shall not stab my soul
And laugh thereafter!　Dark and full of dole
Their bridal feast shall be, most dark the day
They joined their hands, and hunted me away.
　Awake thee now, Medea!　Whatso plot
Thou hast, or cunning, strive and falter not.

On to the peril-point! Now comes the strain
Of daring. Shall they trample thee again?
How? And with Hellas laughing o'er thy fall
While this chief's daughter weds, and weds withal
Jason? . . . A true king was thy father, yea,
And born of the ancient Sun! . . . Thou know'st
    the way;
And God hath made thee woman, things most vain
For help, but wondrous in the paths of pain.

                  [MEDEA *goes into the House.*

CHORUS.

Back streams the wave on the ever-running river:
   Life, life is changed and the laws of it o'ertrod.
Man shall be the slave, the affrighted, the low-liver!
      Man hath forgotten God.
And woman, yea, woman, shall be terrible in story:
   The tales too, meseemeth, shall be other than of
      yore.
For a fear there is that cometh out of Woman and a
      glory,
   And that hard hating voices shall encompass her no
      more!

The old bards shall cease, and their memory that
      lingers
   Of frail brides and faithless, shall be shrivelled as
      with fire.
For they loved us not, nor knew us: and our lips were
      dumb, our fingers
      Could wake not the secret of the lyre.

Else, else, O God the Singer, I had sung amid their
　　rages
　A long tale of Man and his deeds for good and
　　ill.
But the old World knoweth—'tis the speech of all
　　his ages—
　Man's wrong and ours: he knoweth and is still.

Some Women.

Forth from thy father's home
Thou camest, O heart of fire,
To the Dark Blue Rocks, to the clashing foam,
To the seas of thy desire:

Till the Dark Blue Bar was crossed;
And, lo, by an alien river
Standing, thy lover lost,
Void-armed for ever,

Forth yet again, O lowest
Of landless women, a ranger
Of desolate ways, thou goest,
From the walls of the stranger.

Others.

And the great Oath waxeth weak;
And Ruth, as a thing outstriven,
Is fled, fled, from the shores of the Greek,
Away on the winds of heaven.

Dark is the house afar,
    Where an old king called thee daughter;
All that was once thy star
    In stormy water.

Dark: and, lo, in the nearer
    House that was sworn to love thee,
Another, queenlier, dearer,
    Is thronèd above thee.

Enter from the right JASON.

JASON.

Oft have I seen, in other days than these,
How a dark temper maketh maladies
No friend can heal.   'Twas easy to have kept
Both land and home.   It needed but to accept
Unstrivingly the pleasure of our lords.
But thou, for mere delight in stormy words,
Wilt lose all! . . . Now thy speech provokes not me.
Rail on.   Of all mankind let Jason be
Most evil; none shall check thee.   But for these
Dark threats cast out against the majesties
Of Corinth, count as veriest gain thy path
Of exile.   I myself, when princely wrath
Was hot against thee, strove with all good will
To appease the wrath, and wished to keep thee still
Beside me.   But thy mouth would never stay
From vanity, blaspheming night and day
Our masters.   Therefore thou shalt fly the land.
    Yet, even so, I will not hold my hand
From succouring mine own people.   Here am I
To help thee, woman, pondering heedfully

Thy new state.   For I would not have thee flung
Provisionless away—aye, and the young
Children as well; nor lacking aught that will
Of mine can bring thee.   Many a lesser ill
Hangs on the heels of exile.   Aye, and though
Thou hate me, dream not that my heart can know
Or fashion aught of angry will to thee.

MEDEA.

Evil, most evil!   since thou grantest me
That comfort, the worst weapon left me now
To smite a coward   Thou comest to me, thou,
Mine enemy! (*Turning to the* CHORUS.)   Oh, say,
      how call ye this,
To face, and smile, the comrade whom his kiss
Betrayed?   Scorn?   Insult?   Courage?   None of
      these:
'Tis but of all man's inward sicknesses
The vilest, that he knoweth not of shame
Nor pity!   Yet I praise him that he came
To me it shall bring comfort, once to clear
My heart on thee, and thou shalt wince to hear.
   I will begin with that, 'twixt me and thee,
That first befell.   I saved thee.   I saved thee—
Let thine own Greeks be witness, every one
That sailed on Argo—saved thee, sent alone
To yoke with yokes the bulls of fiery breath,
And sow that Acre of the Lords of Death;
And mine own ancient Serpent, who did keep
The Golden Fleece, the eyes that knew not sleep,
And shining coils, him also did I smite
Dead for thy sake, and lifted up the light

That bade thee live.   Myself, uncounsellèd,
Stole forth from father and from home, and fled
Where dark Iôlcos under Pelion lies,
With thee—Oh, single-hearted more than wise!
I murdered Pelias, yea, in agony,
By his own daughters' hands, for sake of thee;
I swept their house like War.—And hast thou then
Accepted all—O evil yet again!—
And cast me off and taken thee for bride
Another?   And with children at thy side!
One could forgive a childless man.   But no:
I have borne thee children . . .

                     Is sworn faith so low
And weak a thing?   I understand it not.
Are the old gods dead?   Are the old laws forgot,
And new laws made?   Since not my passioning,
But thine own heart, doth cry thee for a thing
Forsworn.

> [*She catches sight of her own hand which she
>   has thrown out to denounce him.*

            Poor, poor right hand of mine, whom he
Did cling to, and these knees, so cravingly,
We are unclean, thou and I; we have caught the stain
Of bad men's flesh . . . and dreamed our dreams in
    vain.
   Thou comest to befriend me?   Give me, then,
Thy counsel.   'Tis not that I dream again
For good from thee: but, questioned, thou wilt show
The viler.   Say: now whither shall I go?
Back to my father?   Him I did betray,
And all his land, when we two fled away.
To those poor Peliad maids?   For them 'twere good
To take me in, who spilled their father's blood

Aye, so my whole life stands!   There were at home
Who loved me well: to them I am become
A curse.   And the first friends who sheltered me,
Whom most I should have spared, to pleasure thee
I have turned to foes.   Oh, therefore hast thou laid
My crown upon me, blest of many a maid
In Hellas, now I have won what all did crave,
Thee, the world-wondered lover and the brave;
Who this day looks and sees me banished, thrown
Away with these two babes all, all, alone
Oh, merry mocking when the lamps are red:
" Where go the bridegroom's babes to beg their bread
In exile, and the woman who gave all
To save him? "
            O great God, shall gold withal
Bear thy clear mark, to sift the base and fine,
And o'er man's living visage runs no sign
To show the lie within, ere all too late?

LEADER.

Dire and beyond all healing is the hate
When hearts that loved are turned to enmity.

JASON.

In speech at least, meseemeth, I must be
Not evil; but, as some old pilot goes
Furled to his sail's last edge, when danger blows
Too fiery, run before the wind and swell,
Woman, of thy loud storms.—And thus I tell
My tale.   Since thou wilt build so wondrous high
Thy deeds of service in my jeopardy,

To all my crew and quest I know but one
Saviour, of Gods or mortals one alone,
The Cyprian.   Oh thou hast both brain and wit,
Yet underneath . . . nay, all the tale of it
Were graceless telling; how sheer love, a fire
Of poison-shafts, compelled thee with desire
To save me.   But enough.   I will not score
That count too close.   'Twas good help: and there-
        for
I give thee thanks, howe'er the help was wrought.
Howbeit, in my deliverance, thou hast got
Far more than given.   A good Greek land hath
        been
Thy lasting home, not barbary.   Thou hast seen
Our ordered life, and justice, and the long
Still grasp of law not changing with the strong
Man's pleasure.   Then, all Hellas far and near
Hath learned thy wisdom, and in every ear
Thy fame is.   Had thy days run by unseen
On that last edge of the world, where then had been
The story of great Medea?   Thou and I
What worth to us were treasures heapèd high
In rich kings' rooms; what worth a voice of gold
More sweet than ever rang from Orpheus old,
Unless our deeds have glory?
                              Speak I so,
Touching the Quest I wrought, thyself did throw
The challenge down.   Next for thy cavilling
Of wrath at mine alliance with a king,
Here thou shalt see I both was wise, and free
From touch of passion, and a friend to thee
Most potent, and my children . . . Nay, be still!
    When first I stood in Corinth, clogged with ill

From many a desperate mischance, what bliss
Could I that day have dreamed of, like to this,
To wed with a king's daughter, I exiled
And beggared?   Not—what makes thy passion
     wild—
From loathing of thy bed; not over-fraught
With love for this new bride; not that I sought
To upbuild mine house with offspring: 'tis enough,
What thou hast borne: I make no word thereof:
But, first and greatest, that we all might dwell
In a fair house and want not, knowing well
That poor men have no friends, but far and near
Shunning and silence.   Next, I sought to rear
Our sons in nurture worthy of my race,
And, raising brethren to them, in one place
Join both my houses, and be all from now
Prince-like and happy.   What more need hast
     thou
Of children?   And for me, it serves my star
To link in strength the children that now are
With those that shall be.
                        Have I counselled ill?
Not thine own self would say it, couldst thou still
One hour thy jealous flesh.—'Tis ever so!
Who looks for more in women?   When the flow
Of love runs plain, why, all the world is fair:
But, once there fall some ill chance anywhere
To baulk that thirst, down in swift hate are trod
Men's dearest aims and noblest.   Would to God
We mortals by some other seed could raise
Our fruits, and no blind women block our ways!
Then had there been no curse to wreck man-
     kind.

LEADER.

Lord Jason, very subtly hast thou twined
Thy speech: but yet, though all athwart thy will
I speak, this is not well thou dost, but ill,
Betraying her who loved thee and was true.

MEDEA.

Surely I have my thoughts, and not a few
Have held me strange.   To me it seemeth, when
A crafty tongue is given to evil men
'Tis like to wreck, not help them.   Their own brain
Tempts them with lies to dare and dare again,
Till . . . no man hath enough of subtlety.
As thou—be not so seeming-fair to me
Nor deft of speech.   One word will make thee fall.
Wert thou not false, 'twas thine to tell me all,
And charge me help thy marriage path, as I
Did love thee; not befool me with a lie.

JASON.

An easy task had that been!   Aye, and thou
A loving aid, who canst not, even now,
Still that loud heart that surges like the tide!

MEDEA.

That moved thee not.   Thine old barbarian bride,
The queen out of the east who loved thee sore,
She grew grey-haired, she served thy pride no more.

JASON.

Now understand for once! The girl to me
Is nothing, in this web of sovranty
I hold. I do but seek to save, even yet,
Thee: and for brethren to our sons beget
Young kings, to prosper all our lives again.

MEDEA.

God shelter me from prosperous days of pain,
And wealth that maketh wounds about my heart.

JASON.

Wilt change that prayer, and choose a wiser part?
Pray not to hold true sense for pain, nor rate
Thyself unhappy, being too fortunate.

MEDEA.

Aye, mock me; thou hast where to lay thine head,
But I go naked to mine exile.

JASON.

Tread
Thine own path! Thou hast made it all to be.

MEDEA.

How? By seducing and forsaking thee?

JASON.

By those vile curses on the royal halls
Let loose.

MEDEA.

On thy house also, as chance falls,
I am a living curse.

JASON.

Oh, peace!   Enough
Of these vain wars: I will no more thereof.
If thou wilt take from all that I possess
Aid for these babes and thine own helplessness
Of exile, speak thy bidding.   Here I stand
Full-willed to succour thee with stintless hand,
And send my signet to old friends that dwell
On foreign shores, who will entreat thee well.
Refuse, and thou shalt do a deed most vain.
But cast thy rage away, and thou shalt gain
Much, and lose little for thine anger's sake.

MEDEA.

I will not seek thy friends.   I will not take
Thy givings.   Give them not.   Fruits of a stem
Unholy bring no blessing after them.

JASON.

Now God in heaven be witness, all my heart
Is willing, in all ways, to do its part

For thee and for thy babes.   But nothing good
Can please thee.   In sheer savageness of mood
Thou drivest from thee every friend.   Wherefore
I warrant thee, thy pains shall be the more.

[He goes slowly away.

MEDEA.

Go: thou art weary for the new delight
Thou wooest, so long tarrying out of sight
Of her sweet chamber.   Go, fulfil thy pride,
O bridegroom!   For it may be, such a bride
Shall wait thee,—yea, God heareth me in this—
As thine own heart shall sicken ere it kiss.

CHORUS.

Alas, the Love that falleth like a flood,
     Strong-winged and transitory:
Why praise ye him?   What beareth he of good
     To man, or glory?
Yet Love there is that moves in gentleness,
Heart-filling, sweetest of all powers that bless.
Loose not on me, O Holder of man's heart,
     Thy golden quiver,
Nor steep in poison of desire the dart
     That heals not ever.

The pent hate of the word that cavilleth,
     The strife that hath no fill,
Where once was fondness; and the mad heart's breath
     For strange love panting still:
O Cyprian, cast me not on these; but sift,
Keen-eyed, of love the good and evil gift.

Make Innocence my friend, God's fairest star,
    Yea, and abate not
The rare sweet beat of bosoms without war,
    That love, and hate not.

Others.

Home of my heart, land of my own,
    Cast me not, nay, for pity,
Out on my ways, helpless, alone,
Where the feet fail in the mire and stone,
    A woman without a city.
Ah, not that!   Better the end:
    The green grave cover me rather,
If a break must come in the days I know,
And the skies be changed and the earth below;
For the weariest road that man may wend
    Is forth from the home of his father.

Lo, we have seen: 'tis not a song
    Sung, nor learned of another.
For whom hast thou in thy direst wrong
For comfort?   Never a city strong
    To hide thee, never a brother.
Ah, but the man—cursèd be he,
    Cursèd beyond recover,
Who openeth, shattering, seal by seal,
A friend's clean heart, then turns his heel,
Deaf unto love: never in me
    Friend shall he know nor lover.
[*While* MEDEA *is waiting downcast, seated upon
    her door-step, there passes from the left a
    traveller with followers. As he catches sight
    of* MEDEA *he stops.*

AEGEUS.

Have joy, Medea!   'Tis the homeliest
Word that old friends can greet with, and the best.

MEDEA (*looking up, surprised*).

Oh, joy on thee, too, Aegeus, gentle king
Of Athens!—But whence com'st thou journeying?

AEGEUS.

From Delphi now and the old encaverned stair.

MEDEA.

Where Earth's heart speaks in song?   What mad'st
thou there?

AEGEUS.

Prayed heaven for children—the same search alway.

MEDEA.

Children?   Ah God!   Art childless to this day?

AEGEUS.

So God hath willed.   Childless and desolate.

MEDEA.

What word did Phœbus speak, to change thy fate?

D

AEGEUS.

Riddles, too hard for mortal man to read.

MEDEA.

Which I may hear?

AEGEUS.

           Assuredly they need

A rarer wit.

MEDEA.

How said he?

AEGEUS.

               Not to spill

Life's wine, nor seek for more. · ·

MEDEA.

                  Until?

AEGEUS.

                      Until

I tread the hearth-stone of my sires of yore.

MEDEA.

And what should bring thee here, by Creon's shore?

AEGEUS.

One Pittheus know'st thou, high lord of Trozên?

MEDEA.

Aye, Pelops' son, a man most pure of sin.

AEGEUS.

Him I would ask, touching Apollo's will.

MEDEA.

Much use in God's ways hath he, and much skill.

AEGEUS.

And, long years back he was my battle-friend,
The truest e'er man had.

MEDEA.

Well, may God send
Good hap to thee, and grant all thy desire.

AEGEUS.

But thou   ?   Thy frame is wasted, and the fire
Dead in thine eyes.

MEDEA.

Aegeus, my husband is
The falsest man in the world.

AEGEUS.

What word is this?
Say clearly what thus makes thy visage dim?

MEDEA.

He is false to me, who never injured him.

AEGEUS.

What hath he done?   Show all, that I may see.

MEDEA.

Ta'en him a wife; a wife, set over me
To rule his house!

AEGEUS.

He hath not dared to do,
Jason, a thing so shameful?

MEDEA.

Aye, 'tis true:
And those he loved of yore have no place now.

AEGEUS.

Some passion sweepeth him?   Or is it thou
He turns from?

MEDEA.

Passion, passion to betray
His dearest!

AEGEUS.

Shame be his, so fallen away
From honour!

MEDEA.

Passion to be near a throne,

A king's heir !

AEGEUS.

How, who gives the bride ?　Say on.

MEDEA.

Creon, who o'er all Corinth standeth chief.

AEGEUS.

Woman, thou hast indeed much cause for grief.

MEDEA.

'Tis ruin.—And they have cast me out as well.

AEGEUS.

Who ?　'Tis a new wrong this, and terrible.

MEDEA.

Creon the king, from every land and shore. . . .

AEGEUS.

And Jason suffers him ?　Oh, 'tis too sore !

MEDEA.

He loveth to bear bravely ills like these!
   But, Aegeus, by thy beard, oh, by thy knees,
I pray thee, and I give me for thine own,
Thy suppliant, pity me!   Oh, pity one
So miserable.   Thou never wilt stand there
And see me cast out friendless to despair.
Give me a home in Athens   by the fire
Of thine own hearth!   Oh, so may thy desire
Of children be fulfilled of God, and thou
Die happy! . . . Thou canst know not; even now
Thy prize is won!   I, I will make of thee
A childless man no more.   The seed shall be,
I swear it, sown.   Such magic herbs I know.

AEGEUS.

Woman, indeed my heart goes forth to show
This help to thee, first for religion's sake,
Then for thy promised hope, to heal my ache
Of childlessness   'Tis this hath made mine whole
Life as a shadow, and starved out my soul.
But thus it stands with me.   Once make thy way
To Attic earth, I, as in law I may,
Will keep thee and befriend.   But in this land,
Where Creon rules, I may not raise my hand
To shelter thee.   Move of thine own essay
To seek my house, there thou shalt alway stay,
Inviolate, never to be seized again.
But come thyself from Corinth.   I would fain
Even in foreign eyes be alway just.

MEDEA.

'Tis well.   Give me an oath wherein to trust
And all that man could ask thou hast granted me.

AEGEUS.

Dost trust me not?   Or what thing troubleth thee?

MEDEA.

I trust thee.   But so many, far and near,
Do hate me—all King Pelias' house, and here
Creon.   Once bound by oaths and sanctities
Thou canst not yield me up for such as these
To drag from Athens.   But a spoken word,
No more, to bind thee, which no God hath heard.
The embassies, methinks, would come and go·
They all are friends to thee.   Ah me, I know
Thou wilt not list to me!   So weak am I,
And they full-filled with gold and majesty.

AEGEUS.

Methinks 'tis a far foresight, this thine oath.
Still, if thou so wilt have it, nothing loath
Am I to serve thee.   Mine own hand is so
The stronger, if I have this plea to show
Thy persecutors: and for thee withal
The bond more sure.—On what God shall I call?

MEDEA.

Swear by the Earth thou treadest, by the Sun,
Sire of my sires, and all the gods as one. . . .

AEGEUS.

To do what thing or not do?   Make all plain.

MEDEA.

Never thyself to cast me out again.
Nor let another, whatsoe'er his plea,
Take me, while thou yet livest and art free.

AEGEUS.

Never: so hear me, Earth, and the great star
Of daylight, and all other gods that are!

MEDEA.

'Tis well: and if thou falter from thy vow   .?

AEGEUS.

God's judgment on the godless break my brow!

MEDEA.

Go!   Go thy ways rejoicing.—All is bright
And clear before me.   Go: and ere the night
Myself will follow, when the deed is done
I purpose, and the end I thirst for won.

                              [AEGEUS *and his train depart.*

Chorus.

Farewell: and Maia's guiding Son
   Back lead thee to thy hearth and fire,
   Aegeus; and all the long desire
That wasteth thee, at last be won:
Our eyes have seen thee as thou art,
A gentle and a righteous heart.

Medea.

God, and God's Justice, and ye blinding Skies!
At last the victory dawneth! Yea, mine eyes
See, and my foot is on the mountain's brow.
Mine enemies! Mine enemies, oh, now
Atonement cometh! Here at my worst hour
A friend is found, a very port of power
To save my shipwreck. Here will I make fast
Mine anchor, and escape them at the last
In Athens' walled hill.—But ere the end
'Tis meet I show thee all my counsel, friend:
Take it, no tale to make men laugh withal!
   Straightway to Jason I will send some thrall
To entreat him to my presence. Comes he here,
Then with soft reasons will I feed his ear,
How his will now is my will, how all things
Are well, touching this marriage-bed of kings
For which I am betrayed—all wise and rare
And profitable! Yet will I make one prayer,
That my two children be no more exiled
But stay. . . . Oh, not that I would leave a child

Here upon angry shores till those have laughed
Who hate me: 'tis that I will slay by craft
The king's daughter.   With gifts they shall be sent,
Gifts to the bride to spare their banishment,
Fine robings and a carcanet of gold.
Which raiment let her once but take, and fold
About her, a foul death that girl shall die
And all who touch her in her agony.
Such poison shall they drink, my robe and wreath!
    Howbeit, of that no more.   I gnash my teeth
Thinking on what a path my feet must tread
Thereafter.   I shall lay those children dead—
Mine, whom no hand shall steal from me away!
Then, leaving Jason childless, and the day
As night above him, I will go my road
To exile, flying, flying from the blood
Of these my best-beloved, and having wrought
All horror, so but one thing reach me not,
The laugh of them that hate us.
                                          Let it come!
What profits life to me?   I have no home,
No country now, nor shield from any wrong.
That was my evil hour, when down the long
Halls of my father out I stole, my will
Chained by a Greek man's voice, who still, oh, still,
If God yet live, shall all requited be.
For never child of mine shall Jason see
Hereafter living, never child beget
From his new bride, who this day, desolate
Even as she made me desolate, shall die
Shrieking amid my poisons. . . . Names have I
Among your folk?   One light?   One weak of hand?
An eastern dreamer?—Nay, but with the brand

Of strange suns burnt, my hate, by God above,
A perilous thing, and passing sweet my love!
For these it is that make life glorious.

LEADER.

Since thou hast bared thy fell intent to us
I, loving thee, and helping in their need
Man's laws, adjure thee, dream not of this deed!

MEDEA.

There is no other way.—I pardon thee
Thy littleness, who art not wronged like me.

LEADER.

Thou canst not kill the fruit thy body bore!

MEDEA.

Yes: if the man I hate be pained the more.

LEADER.

And thou made miserable, most miserable?

MEDEA.

Oh, let it come! All words of good or ill
Are wasted now.
      [*She claps her hands: the* NURSE *comes out from
         the house.*
                     Ho, woman; get thee gone
And lead lord Jason hither.   There is none

Like thee, to work me these high services.
But speak no word of what my purpose is,
As thou art faithful, thou, and bold to try
All succours, and a woman even as I!

[*The* NURSE *departs.*

CHORUS.

The sons of Erechtheus, the olden,
  Whom high gods planted of yore
In an old land of heaven upholden,
  A proud land untrodden of war:
They are hungered, and, lo, their desire
  With wisdom is fed as with meat:
In their skies is a shining of fire,
  A joy in the fall of their feet:
And thither, with manifold dowers,
  From the North, from the hills, from the morn,
The Muses did gather their powers,
  That a child of the Nine should be born;
And Harmony, sown as the flowers,
  Grew gold in the acres of corn.

And Cephîsus, the fair-flowing river—
  The Cyprian dipping her hand
Hath drawn of his dew, and the shiver
  Of her touch is as joy in the land.
For her breathing in fragrance is written,
  And in music her path as she goes,
And the cloud of her hair, it is litten
  With stars of the wind-woven rose.
So fareth she ever and ever,
  And forth of her bosom is blown,

As dews on the winds of the river,
  An hunger of passions unknown,
Strong Loves of all godlike endeavour,
  Whom Wisdom shall throne on her throne.

Some Women.

But Cephîsus the fair-flowing,
  Will he bear thee on his shore?
   Shall the land that succours all, succour thee,
Who art foul among thy kind,
With the tears of children blind?
Dost thou see the red gash growing,
   Thine own burden dost thou see?
    Every side, Every way,
  Lo, we kneel to thee and pray:
   By thy knees, by thy soul, O woman wild!
One at least thou canst not slay,
    Not thy child!

Others.

Hast thou ice that thou shalt bind it
  To thy breast, and make thee dead
   To thy children, to thine own spirit's pain?
When the hand knows what it dares,
When thine eyes look into theirs,
Shalt thou keep by tears unblinded
   Thy dividing of the slain?
    These be deeds Not for thee:
  These be things that cannot be!
   Thy babes—though thine hardihood be fell,
When they cling about thy knee,
    'Twill be well!

Enter JASON.

JASON.

I answer to thy call.   Though full of hate
Thou be, I yet will not so far abate
My kindness for thee, nor refuse mine ear.
Say in what new desire thou hast called me here.

MEDEA.

Jason, I pray thee, for my words but now
Spoken, forgive me.   My bad moods. . .   Oh, thou
At least wilt strive to bear with them!   There be
Many old deeds of love 'twixt me and thee.
Lo, I have reasoned with myself apart
And chidden: "Why must I be mad, O heart
Of mine: and raging against one whose word
Is wisdom: making me a thing abhorred
To them that rule the land, and to mine own
Husband, who doth but that which, being done,
Will help us all—to wed a queen, and get
Young kings for brethren to my sons?   And yet
I rage alone, and cannot quit my rage—
What aileth me?—when God sends harbourage
So simple?   Have I not my children?   Know
I not we are but exiles, and must go
Beggared and   friendless   else?"   Thought   upon
    thought
So pressed me, till I knew myself full-fraught
With bitterness of heart and blinded eyes.
So now—I give thee thanks: and hold thee wise

To have caught this anchor for our aid.   The fool
Was I; who should have been thy friend, thy tool;
Gone wooing with thee, stood at thy bed-side
Serving, and welcomed duteously thy bride.
But, as we are, we are—I will not say
Mere evil—women!   Why must thou to-day
Turn strange, and make thee like some evil thing,
Childish, to meet my childish passioning?
See, I surrender: and confess that then
I had bad thoughts, but now have turned again
And found my wiser mind.   [*She claps her hands.*
                              Ho, children!   Run
Quickly!   Come hither, out into the sun,
    [*The* CHILDREN *come from the house, followed by
        their* ATTENDANT.
And greet your father.   Welcome him with us,
And throw quite, quite away, as mother does,
Your anger against one so dear.   Our peace
Is made, and all the old bad war shall cease
For ever.—Go, and take his hand.
    [*As the* CHILDREN *go to* JASON, *she suddenly
        bursts into tears. The* CHILDREN *quickly
        return to her: she recovers herself, smiling
        amid her tears.*
                              Ah me,
I am full of hidden horrors! . . . Shall it be
A long time more, my children, that ye live
To reach to me those dear, dear arms? . . . Forgive!
I am so ready with my tears to-day,
And full of dread. . . . I sought to smooth away
The long strife with your father, and, lo, now
I have all drowned with tears this little brow!
                        [*She wipes the child's face.*

LEADER.

O'er mine eyes too there stealeth a pale tear:
Let the evil rest, O God, let it rest here!

JASON.

Woman, indeed I praise thee now, nor say
Ill of thine other hour.   'Tis nature's way,
A woman needs must stir herself to wrath,
When work of marriage by so strange a path
Crosseth her lord.   But thou, thine heart doth wend
The happier road.   Thou hast seen, ere quite the end,
What choice must needs be stronger: which to do
Shows a wise-minded woman. . . . And for you,
Children; your father never has forgot
Your needs.   If God but help him, he hath wrought
A strong deliverance for your weakness.   Yea,
I think you, with your brethren, yet one day
Shall be the mightiest voices in this land.
Do you grow tall and strong.   Your father's hand
Guideth all else, and whatso power divine
Hath alway helped him. . . . Ah, may it be mine
To see you yet in manhood, stern of brow,
Strong-armed, set high o'er those that hate me. . .
                                                    How?
Woman, thy face is turned.   Thy cheek is swept
With pallor of strange tears.   Dost not accept
Gladly and of good will my benisons?

MEDEA.

'Tis nothing.   Thinking of these little ones.   . .

JASON.

Take heart, then.   I will guard them from all ill.

MEDEA.

I do take heart.   Thy word I never will
Mistrust.   Alas, a woman's bosom bears
But woman's courage, a thing born for tears.

JASON.

What ails thee?—All too sore thou weepest there.

MEDEA.

I was their mother!   When I heard thy prayer
Of long life for them, there swept over me
A horror, wondering how these things shall be.
    But for the matter of my need that thou
Should speak with me, part I have said, and now
Will finish.—Seeing it is the king's behest
To cast me out from Corinth . . . aye, and best,
Far best, for me—I know it—not to stay
Longer to trouble thee and those who sway
The realm, being held to all their house a foe. . . .
Behold, I spread my sails, and meekly go

E

To exile.   But our children. . .   Could this land
Be still their home awhile: could thine own hand
But guide their boyhood. . . . Seek the king, and
    pray
His pity, that he bid thy children stay!

JASON.

He is hard to move.   Yet surely 'twere well done.

MEDEA.

Bid h e r—for thy sake, for a daughter's boon. . . .

JASON.

Well thought!   Her I can fashion to my mind.

MEDEA.

Surely.   She is a woman like her kind. . . .
Yet I will aid thee in thy labour; I
Will send her gifts, the fairest gifts that lie
In the hands of men, things of the days of old,
Fine robings and a carcanet of gold,
By the boys' hands.—Go, quick, some handmaiden,
And fetch the raiment.
              [*A handmaid goes into the house.*
          Ah, her cup shall then
Be filled indeed!   What more should woman crave,
Being wed with thee, the bravest of the brave,

And girt with raiment which of old the sire
Of all my house, the Sun, gave, steeped in fire,
To his own fiery race?

    [*The handmaid has returned bearing the Gifts.*
                Come, children, lift
With heed these caskets.　Bear them as your gift
To her, being bride and princess and of right
Blessed!—I think she will not hold them light.

JASON.

Fond woman, why wilt empty thus thine hand
Of treasure?　Doth King Creon's castle stand
In stint of raiment, or in stint of gold?
Keep these, and make no gift.　For if she hold
Jason of any worth at all, I swear
Chattels like these will not weigh more with her.

MEDEA.

Ah, chide me not!　'Tis written, gifts persuade
The gods in heaven; and gold is stronger made
Than words innumerable to bend men's ways.
Fortune is hers.　God maketh great her days:
Young and a crownèd queen!　And banishment
For those two babes. . . . I would not gold were
    spent,
But life's blood, ere that come.

                    My children, go
Forth into those rich halls, and, bowing low,
Beseech your father's bride, whom I obey,
Ye be not, of her mercy, cast away

Exiled: and give the caskets—above all
Mark this!—to none but her, to hold withal
And keep. . . . Go quick! And let your mother
    know
Soon the good tidings that she longs for. . . . Go!
    [*She goes quickly into the house.* JASON *and the*
        CHILDREN *with their* ATTENDANT *depart.*

CHORUS.

Now I have no hope more of the children's living;
    No hope more.   They are gone forth unto death.
The bride, she taketh the poison of their giving:
    She taketh the bounden gold and openeth;
And the crown, the crown, she lifteth about her brow,
Where the light brown curls are clustering.   No
    hope now!

O sweet and cloudy gleam of the garments golden!
    The robe, it hath clasped her breast and the crown
        her head.
Then, then, she decketh the bride, as a bride of
    olden
    Story, that goeth pale to the kiss of the dead.
For the ring hath closed, and the portion of death
    is there;
And she flieth not, but perisheth unaware.

Some Women.

O bridegroom, bridegroom of the kiss so cold,
Art thou wed with princes, art thou girt with gold,

Who know'st not, suing
For thy child's undoing,
And, on her thou lovest, for a doom untold?
How art thou fallen from thy place of old!

Others.

O Mother, Mother, what hast thou to reap,
When the harvest cometh, between wake and sleep?
For a heart unslaken,
For a troth forsaken,
Lo, babes that call thee from a bloody deep:
And thy love returns not.   Get thee forth and weep!
[*Enter the* ATTENDANT *with the two* CHILDREN:
MEDEA *comes out from the house.*

ATTENDANT.

Mistress, these children from their banishment
Are spared.   The royal bride hath mildly bent
Her hand to accept thy gifts, and all is now
Peace for the children.—Ha, why standest thou
Confounded, when good fortune draweth near?

MEDEA.

Ah God!

ATTENDANT.

This chimes not with the news I bear.

MEDEA.

O God, have mercy!

ATTENDANT.

Is some word of wrath
Here hidden that I knew not of?   And hath
My hope to give thee joy so cheated me?

MEDEA.

Thou givest what thou givest: I blame not thee.

ATTENDANT.

Thy brows are all o'ercast: thine eyes are filled.   . .

MEDEA.

For bitter need, Old Man!   The gods have willed,
And mine own evil mind, that this should come.

ATTENDANT.

Take heart!   Thy sons one day will bring thee home.

MEDEA.

Home?   I have others to send home.   Woe's me!

ATTENDANT.

Be patient.   Many a mother before thee
Hath parted from her children.   We poor things
Of men must needs endure what fortune brings.

MEDEA.

I will endure.—Go thou within, and lay
All ready that my sons may need to-day.

[*The* ATTENDANT *goes into the house.*

O children, children mine: and you have found
A land and home, where, leaving me discrowned
And desolate, for ever you will stay,
Motherless children!   And I go my way
To other lands, an exile, ere you bring
Your fruits home, ere I see you prospering
Or know your brides, or deck the bridal bed,
All flowers, and lift your torches overhead.

   Oh, cursèd be mine own hard heart!   'Twas all
In vain, then, that I reared you up, so tall
And fair; in vain I bore you, and was torn
With those long pitiless pains, when you were
   born.
Ah, wondrous hopes my poor heart had in you,
How you would tend me in mine age, and do
The shroud about me with your own dear hands,
When I lay cold, blessèd in all the lands
That knew us.   And that gentle thought is dead!
You go, and I live on, to eat the bread
Of long years, to myself most full of pain.
And never your dear eyes, never again,
Shall see your mother, far away being thrown
To other shapes of life   My babes, my own,
Why gaze ye so?—What is it that ye see?—
And laugh with that last laughter? . . . Woe is me,
What shall I do?

                    Women, my strength is gone,
Gone like a dream, since once I looked upon

Those shining faces. . . . I can do it not.
Good-bye to all the thoughts that burned so hot
Aforetime!   I will take and hide them far,
Far, from men's eyes.   Why should I seek a war
So blind: by these babes' wounds to sting again
Their father's heart, and win myself a pain
Twice deeper?   Never, never!   I forget
Henceforward all I laboured for.

                        And yet,
What is it with me?   Would I be a thing
Mocked at, and leave mine enemies to sting
Unsmitten?   It must be.   O coward heart,
Ever to harbour such soft words!—Depart
Out of my sight, ye twain.   [*The* CHILDREN *go in.*
                    And they whose eyes
Shall hold it sin to share my sacrifice,
On their heads be it!   My hand shall swerve not
    now.

   Ah, Ah, thou Wrath within me!   Do not thou,
Do not. . . . Down, down, thou tortured thing, and
    spare
My children!   They will dwell with us, aye, there
Far off, and give thee peace.
                  Too late, too late!
By all Hell's living agonies of hate,
They shall not take my little ones alive
To make their mock with!   Howsoe'er I strive
The thing is doomed; it shall not escape now
From being.   Aye, the crown is on the brow,
And the robe girt, and in the robe that high
Queen dying
             I know all.   Yet . . . seeing that I

Must go so long a journey, and these twain
A longer yet and darker, I would fain
Speak with them, ere I go.
> [*A handmaid brings the* CHILDREN *out again.*
　　　　　　　　　　Come, children; stand
A little from me.　There.　Reach out your hand,
Your right hand—so—to mother: and good-bye!
> [*She has kept them hitherto at arm's-length: but*
> *at the touch of their hands, her resolution*
> *breaks down, and she gathers them pas-*
> *sionately into her arms.*

Oh, darling hand!　Oh, darling mouth, and eye,
And royal mien, and bright brave faces clear,
May you be blessèd, but not here!　What here
Was yours, your father stole. . . . Ah God, the glow
Of cheek on cheek, the tender touch; and Oh,
Sweet scent of childhood. . . . Go! Go! . .　Am I
　　blind? . . .
Mine eyes can see not, when I look to find
Their places.　I am broken by the wings
Of evil. . . . Yea, I know to what bad things
I go, but louder than all thought doth cry
Anger, which maketh man's worst misery.
> [*She follows the* CHILDREN *into the house.*

CHORUS.

> My thoughts have roamed a cloudy land,
> And heard a fierier music fall
> Than woman's heart should stir withal:
> And yet some Muse majestical,
> Unknown, hath hold of woman's hand,
> Seeking for Wisdom—not in all:

A feeble seed, a scattered band,
Thou yet shalt find in lonely places,
Not dead amongst us, nor our faces
Turned alway from the Muses' call.

And thus my thought would speak: that she
Who ne'er hath borne a child nor known
Is nearer to felicity:
Unlit she goeth and alone,
With little understanding what
A child's touch means of joy or woe,
And many toils she beareth not.

But they within whose garden fair
That gentle plant hath blown, they go
Deep-written all their days with care—
To rear the children, to make fast
Their hold, to win them wealth; and then
Much darkness, if the seed at last
Bear fruit in good or evil men!
And one thing at the end of all
Abideth, that which all men dread:
The wealth is won, the limbs are bred
To manhood, and the heart withal
Honest: and, lo, where Fortune smiled,
Some change, and what hath fallen?   Hark!
'Tis death slow winging to the dark,
And in his arms what was thy child.

What therefore doth it bring of gain
To man, whose cup stood full before,

That God should send this one thing more
Of hunger and of dread, a door
Set wide to every wind of pain?

[MEDEA *comes out alone from the hou*

MEDEA.

Friends, this long hour I wait on Fortune's eyes,
And strain my senses in a hot surmise
What passeth on that hill.—Ha! even now
There comes   'tis one of Jason's men, I trow.
His wild-perturbèd breath doth warrant me
The tidings of some strange calamity.

[*Enter* MESSENGER.

MESSENGER.

O dire and ghastly deed!   Get thee away,
Medea!   Fly!   Nor let behind thee stay
One chariot's wing, one keel that sweeps the seas.

MEDEA.

And what hath chanced, to cause such flights as these?

MESSENGER.

The maiden princess lieth—and her sire,
The king—both murdered by thy poison-fire.

MEDEA.

Most happy tiding!   Which thy name prefers
Henceforth among my friends and well-wishers.

MESSENGER.

What say'st thou?   Woman, is thy mind within
Clear, and not raving?   Thou art found in sin
Most bloody wrought against the king's high head,
And laughest at the tale, and hast no dread?

MEDEA.

I have words also that could answer well
Thy word.   But take thine ease, good friend, and tell,
How died they?   Hath it been a very foul
Death, prithee?   That were comfort to my soul.

MESSENGER.

When thy two children, hand in hand entwined,
Came with their father, and passed on to find
The new-made bridal rooms, Oh, we were glad,
We thralls, who ever loved thee well, and had
Grief in thy grief.   And straight there passed a word
From ear to ear, that thou and thy false lord
Had poured peace offering upon wrath foregone.
A right glad welcome gave we them, and one
Kissed the small hand, and one the shining hair:
Myself, for very joy, I followed where
The women's rooms are.   There our mistress . . . she
Whom now we name so . . . thinking not to see
Thy little pair, with glad and eager brow
Sate waiting Jason.   Then she saw, and slow
Shrouded her eyes, and backward turned again,
Sick that thy children should come near her.   Then

Thy husband quick went forward, to entreat
The young maid's fitful wrath. " Thou wilt not
        meet
Love's coming with unkindness? Nay, refrain
Thy suddenness, and turn thy face again,
Holding as friends all that to me are dear,
Thine husband. And accept these robes they bear
As gifts: and beg thy father to unmake
His doom of exile on them—for my sake."
When once she saw the raiment, she could still
Her joy no more, but gave him all his will.
And almost ere the father and the two
Children were gone from out the room, she drew
The flowerèd garments forth, and sate her down
To her arraying: bound the golden crown
Through her long curls, and in a mirror fair
Arranged their separate clusters, smiling there
At the dead self that faced her. Then aside
She pushed her seat, and paced those chambers
        wide
Alone, her white foot poising delicately—
So passing joyful in those gifts was she!—
And many a time would pause, straight-limbed, and
        wheel.
Her head to watch the long fold to her heel
Sweeping. And then came something strange. Her
        cheek
Seemed pale, and back with crooked steps and
        weak
Groping of arms she walked, and scarcely found
Her old seat, that she fell not to the ground.
    Among the handmaids was a woman old
And grey, who deemed, I think, that Pan had hold

Upon her, or some spirit, and raised a keen
Awakening shout; till through her lips was seen
A white foam crawling, and her eyeballs back
Twisted, and all her face dead pale for lack
Of life: and while that old dame called, the cry
Turned strangely to its opposite, to die
Sobbing. Oh, swiftly then one woman flew
To seek her father's rooms, one for the new
Bridegroom, to tell the tale. And all the place
Was loud with hurrying feet.

                       So long a space
As a swift walker on a measured way
Would pace a furlong's course in, there she lay
Speechless, with veilèd lids. Then wide her eyes
She oped, and wildly, as she strove to rise,
Shrieked: for two diverse waves upon her rolled
Of stabbing death. The carcanet of gold
That gripped her brow was molten in a dire
And wondrous river of devouring fire.
And those fine robes, the gift thy children gave—
God's mercy!—everywhere did lap and lave
The delicate flesh; till up she sprang, and fled,
A fiery pillar, shaking locks and head
This way and that, seeking to cast the crown
Somewhere away. But like a thing nailed down
The burning gold held fast the anadem,
And through her locks, the more she scattered
    them,
Came fire the fiercer, till to earth she fell
A thing—save to her sire—scarce nameable,
And strove no more. That cheek of royal mien,
Where was it—or the place where eyes had
    been?

Only from crown and temples came faint blood
Shot through with fire.   The very flesh, it stood
Out from the bones, as from a wounded pine
The gum starts, where those gnawing poisons fine
Bit in the dark—a ghastly sight!   And touch
The dead we durst not.   We had seen too much.

But that poor father, knowing not, had sped,
Swift to his daughter's room, and there the dead
Lay at his feet.   He knelt, and groaning low,
Folded her in his arms, and kissed her: " Oh,
Unhappy child, what thing unnatural hath
So hideously undone thee?   Or what wrath
Of gods, to make this old grey sepulchre
Childless of thee?   Would God but lay me there
To die with thee, my daughter!"   So he cried.
But after, when he stayed from tears, and tried
To uplift his old bent frame, lo, in the folds
Of those fine robes it held, as ivy holds
Strangling among young laurel boughs.   Oh, then
A ghastly struggle came.   Again, again,
Up on his knee he writhed; but that dead breast
Clung still to his: till, wild, like one possessed,
He dragged himself half free; and, lo, the live
Flesh parted; and he laid him down to strive
No more with death, but perish; for the deep
Had risen above his soul.   And there they sleep,
At last, the old proud father and the bride,
Even as his tears had craved it, side by side.

For thee—Oh, no word more! Thyself will
     know
How best to baffle vengeance. . . . Long ago
I looked upon man's days, and found a grey
Shadow.   And this thing more I surely say,

That those of all men who are counted wise,
Strong wits, devisers of great policies,
Do pay the bitterest toll.   Since life began,
Hath there in God's eye stood one happy man?
Fair days roll on, and bear more gifts or less
Of fortune, but to no man happiness.

[*Exit* MESSENGER.

CHORUS.

Some Women.

Wrath upon wrath, meseems, this day shall fall
From God on Jason!   He hath earned it all.

Other Women.

O miserable maiden, all my heart
Is torn for thee, so sudden to depart
From thy king's chambers and the light above
To darkness, all for sake of Jason's love!

MEDEA.

Women, my mind is clear.   I go to slay
My children with all speed, and then, away
From hence; not wait yet longer till they stand
Beneath another and an angrier hand
To die.   Yea, howsoe'er I shield them, die
They must.   And, seeing that they must, 'tis I
Shall slay them, I their mother, touched of none
Beside.   Oh, up, and get thine armour on,

My heart!   Why longer tarry we to win
Our crown of dire inevitable sin?
Take up thy sword, O poor right hand of mine,
Thy sword: then onward to the thin-drawn line
Where life turns agony.   Let there be naught
Of softness now: and keep thee from that thought,
"Born of thy flesh," "thine own belovèd."   Now,
For one brief day, forget thy children: thou
Shalt weep hereafter.   Though thou slay them, yet
Sweet were they. . . . I am sore unfortunate.

[*She goes into the house.*

CHORUS.

Some Women.

O Earth, our mother; and thou
  All-seër, arrowy crown
Of Sunlight, manward now
  Look down, Oh, look down!
Look upon one accurst,
  Ere yet in blood she twine
  Red hands—blood that is thine!
O Sun, save her first!
She is thy daughter still,
  Of thine own golden line;
Save her!   Or shall man spill
    The life divine?
Give peace, O Fire that diest not!   Send thy spell
  To stay her yet, to lift her afar, afar—
A torture-changèd spirit, a voice of Hell
  Wrought of old wrongs and war!

F

Others.

Alas for the mother's pain
    Wasted! Alas the dear
Life that was born in vain!
    Woman, what mak'st thou here,
Thou from beyond the Gate
    Where dim Symplêgades
    Clash in the dark blue seas,
The shores where death doth wait?
Why hast thou taken on thee,
    To make us desolate,
This anger of misery
    And guilt of hate?
For fierce are the smitings back of blood once shed
  Where love hath been: God's wrath upon them
    that kill,
And an anguished earth, and the wonder of the dead
  Haunting as music still. . . .
                [A cry is heard within.

A Woman.

Hark! Did ye hear? Heard ye the children's cry?

Another.

O miserable woman! O abhorred!

A Child within.

What shall I do? What is it? Keep me fast
From mother!

The Other Child.

      I know nothing. Brother! Oh,
I think she means to kill us.

A Woman.

Let me go!
I will—Help!   Help!—and save them at the
   last.

A Child.
Yes, in God's name!   Help quickly ere we die!

The Other Child.
She has almost caught me now.   She has a sword.
[*Many of the Women are now beating at the
   barred door to get in.   Others are standing
   apart.*

Women at the door.
Thou stone, thou thing of iron!   Wilt verily
Spill with thine hand that life, the vintage stored
   Of thine own agony?

The Other Women.
A Mother slew her babes in days of yore,
   One, only one, from dawn to eventide,
      Ino, god-maddened, whom the Queen of Heaven
         Set frenzied, flying to the dark: and she
         Cast her for sorrow to the wide salt sea,
      Forth from those rooms of murder unforgiven,
Wild-footed from a white crag of the shore,
   And clasping still her children twain, she died.

O Love of Woman, charged with sorrow sore,
   What hast thou wrought upon us?   What beside
      Resteth to tremble for?
         [*Enter hurriedly* JASON *and Attendants.*

JASON.

Ye women by this doorway clustering
Speak, is the doer of the ghastly thing
Yet here, or fled?   What hopeth she of flight?
Shall the deep yawn to shield her?   Shall the height
Send wings, and hide her in the vaulted sky
To work red murder on her lords, and fly
Unrecompensed?   But let her go!   My care
Is but to save my children, not for her.
Let them she wronged requite her as they may.
I care not.   'Tis my sons I must some way
Save, ere the kinsmen of the dead can win
From them the payment of their mother's sin.

LEADER.

Unhappy man, indeed thou knowest not
What dark place thou art come to!   Else, God
        wot,
Jason, no word like these could fall from thee.

JASON.

What is it!—Ha!   The woman would kill me?

LEADER.

Thy sons are dead, slain by their mother's hand.

JASON.

How?   Not the children. .   I scarce under-
        stand. .
O God, thou hast broken me!

LEADER.

Think of those twain
As things once fair, that ne'er shall bloom again.

JASON.

Where did she murder them? In that old room?

LEADER.

Open, and thou shalt see thy children's doom.

JASON.

Ho, thralls! Unloose me yonder bars! Make more
Of speed! Wrench out the jointing of the door.
And show my two-edged curse, the children dead,
The woman. . . . Oh, this sword upon her
    head
    [*While the Attendants are still battering at the
        door* MEDEA *appears on the roof, standing
        on a chariot of winged Dragons, in which are
        the children's bodies.*

MEDEA.

What make ye at my gates? Why batter ye
With brazen bars, seeking the dead and me
Who slew them? Peace! . . . And thou, if aught
    of mine
Thou needest, speak, though never touch of thine

Shall scathe me more.   Out of his firmament
My fathers' father, the high Sun, hath sent
This, that shall save me from mine enemies' rage.

JASON.

Thou living hate!   Thou wife in every age
Abhorrèd, blood-red mother, who didst kill
My sons, and make me as the dead: and still
Canst take the sunshine to thine eyes, and smell
The green earth, reeking from thy deed of hell;
I curse thee! Now, Oh, now mine eyes can see,
That then were blinded, when from savagery
Of eastern chambers, from a cruel land,
To Greece and home I gathered in mine hand
Thee, thou incarnate curse: one that betrayed
Her home, her father, her . . . Oh, God hath
      laid
Thy sins on me!—I knew, I knew, there lay
A brother murdered on thy hearth that day
When thy first footstep fell on Argo's hull. . . .
Argo, my own, my swift and beautiful!
    That was her first beginning.   Then a wife
I made her in my house.   She bore to life
Children: and now for love, for chambering
And men's arms, she hath murdered them!   A
      thing
Not one of all the maids of Greece, not one,
Had dreamed of; whom I spurned, and for mine
      own
Chose thee, a bride of hate to me and death,
Tigress, not woman, beast of wilder breath

Than Skylla shrieking o'er the Tuscan sea.
Enough!   No scorn of mine can reach to thee,
Such iron is o'er thine eyes.   Out from my road,
Thou crime-begetter, blind with children's blood!
And let me weep alone the bitter tide
That sweepeth Jason's days, no gentle bride
To speak with more, no child to look upon
Whom once I reared . . . all, all for ever gone!

MEDEA.

An easy answer had I to this swell
Of speech, but Zeus our father knoweth well,
All I for thee have wrought, and thou for me.
So let it rest.   This thing was not to be,
That thou shouldst live a merry life, my bed
Forgotten and my heart uncomforted,
Thou nor thy princess: nor the king that planned
Thy marriage drive Medea from his land,
And suffer not.   Call me what thing thou please,
Tigress or Skylla from the Tuscan seas:
My claws have gripped thine heart, and all things
    shine.

JASON.

Thou too hast grief.   Thy pain is fierce as mine.

MEDEA.

I love the pain, so thou shalt laugh no more.

JASON.

Oh, what a womb of sin my children bore!

MEDEA.

Sons, did ye perish for your father's shame?

JASON.

How?   It was not my hand that murdered them.

MEDEA.

'Twas thy false wooings, 'twas thy trampling pride.

JASON.

Thou hast said it!   For thy lust of love they died.

MEDEA.

And love to women a slight thing should be?

JASON.

To women pure!—All thy vile life to thee!

MEDEA.

Think of thy torment.   They are dead, they are dead!

JASON.

No: quick, great God; quick curses round thy head!

MEDEA.

The Gods know who began this work of woe.

JASON.

Thy heart and all its loathliness they know.

MEDEA.

Loathe on. . .   But, Oh, thy voice.   It hurts me
    sore.

JASON.

Aye, and thine me.   Wouldst hear me then no more?

MEDEA.

How?   Show me but the way.   'Tis this I crave.

JASON.

Give me the dead to weep, and make their grave.

MEDEA.

Never!   Myself will lay them in a still
Green sepulchre, where Hera by the Hill
Hath precinct holy, that no angry men
May break their graves and cast them forth again
To evil.   So I lay on all this shore
Of Corinth a high feast for evermore
And rite, to purge them yearly of the stain
Of this poor blood.   And I, to Pallas' plain
I go, to dwell beside Pandion's son,
Aegeus.—For thee, behold, death draweth on,
Evil and lonely, like thine heart: the hands
Of thine old Argo, rotting where she stands,

Shall smite thine head in twain, and bitter be
To the last end thy memories of me.
    [*She rises on the chariot and is slowly borne away.*

JASON.

May They that hear the weeping child
  Blast thee, and They that walk in blood!

MEDEA.

Thy broken vows, thy friends beguiled
  Have shut for thee the ears of God.

JASON.

Go, thou art wet with children's tears!

MEDEA.

Go thou, and lay thy bride to sleep.

JASON.

Childless, I go, to weep and weep.

MEDEA.

Not yet!   Age cometh and long years.

JASON.

My sons, mine own!
          MEDEA.
               Not thine, but mine

JASON.

. . . Who slew them!

MEDEA.

            Yes: to torture thee.

JASON.

Once let me kiss their lips, once twine
    Mine arms, and touch. . . . Ah, woe is me!

MEDEA.

Wouldst love them and entreat?   But now
    They were as nothing.

JASON.

                              At the last.
O God, to touch that tender brow!

MEDEA.

Thy words upon the wind are cast.

JASON.

Thou, Zeus, wilt hear me.   All is said
    For naught. I am but spurned away
And trampled by this tigress, red
    With children's blood.   Yet, come what may,
So far as thou hast granted, yea,
    So far as yet my strength may stand,
I weep upon these dead, and say
    Their last farewell, and raise my hand

To all the daemons of the air
    In witness of these things; how she
    Who slew them, will not suffer me
To gather up my babes, nor bear
To earth their bodies; whom, O stone
Of women, would I ne'er had known
    Nor gotten, to be slain by thee!
            [He casts himself upon the earth.

CHORUS.

Great treasure halls hath Zeus in heaven,
From whence to man strange dooms be given,
       Past hope or fear.
And the end men looked for cometh not,
And a path is there where no man thought:
       So hath it fallen here.

P. 3, l. 2, To Colchis through the blue Symplê-gades.]—The Symplêgades (" Clashing ") or Kuaneai (" Dark blue ") were two rocks in the sea which used to clash together and crush anything that was be-tween them. They stood above the north end of the Bosphorus and formed the Gate (l. 1264, p. 70) to the Axeinos Pontos, or '· Stranger-less Sea," where all Greeks were murdered. At the farthest eastern end of that sea was the land of Colchis.

P. 3, l. 3, Pêlion.]—The great mountain in Thessaly. Iôlcos, a little kingdom between Pêlion and the sea, ruled originally by Aeson, Jason's father, then by the usurping Pĕlias.

P. 3, l. 9, Daughters of Pĕlias.]—See Introduction, p. vii.

P. 4, l. 18, Wed.]—Medea was not legally married to Jason, and could not be, though in common par-lance he is sometimes called her husband. Inter-marriage between the subjects of two separate states was not possible in antiquity without a special treaty. And naturally there was no such treaty with Colchis.

This is, I think, the view of the play, and corre-sponds to the normal Athenian conceptions of society. In the original legend it is likely enough that Medea belongs to " matriarchal " times before the institution of marriage.

P. 4, l. 18, Head of Corinth.]—A peculiar word

(αἰσυμναν) afterwards used to translate the Roman *dictator*. Creon is, however, apparently descended from the ancient king Sisyphus.

P. 4, l. 40, She hath a blade made keen, &c.]— These lines (40, 41) are repeated in a different context later on, p. 23, ll. 379, 380. The sword which to the Nurse suggested suicide was really meant for murder. There is a similar and equally dramatic repetition of the lines about the crown and wreath (786, 949, pp. 46, 54), and of those about the various characters popularly attributed to Medea (ll. 304, 808, pp. 18, 46).

P. 5, l. 48, ATTENDANT.]—Greek *Paidagôgos*, or "pedagogue"; a confidential servant who escorted the boys to and from school, and in similar ways looked after them. Notice the rather light and cynical character of this man, compared with the tenderness of the Nurse.

P. 5, l. 57, To this still earth and sky]—Not a mere stage explanation. It was the ancient practice, if you had bad dreams or terrors of the night, to "show" them to the Sun in the morning, that he might clear them away.

P. 8, l. 111, Have I not suffered?]—Medea is apparently answering some would-be comforter. Cf. p. 4. (" If friends will speak," &c.)

P. 9, l. 131, CHORUS.]—As Dr. Verrall has remarked, the presence of the Chorus is in this play unusually awkward from the dramatic point of view. Medea's plot demands most absolute secrecy; and it is incredible that fifteen Corinthian women, simply because they were women, should allow a half-mad foreigner to murder several people, including their own Corinthian king and princess—who was a woman also — rather than reveal her plot   We must remember in palliation (1) that these women belong to the faction in Corinth which was friendly to Medea and hostile to Creon; (2) that the appeal to them as women had more force in antiquity than it would now, and the princess had really turned traitor to her sex.   (See note on this subject at the end of the present writer's translation of the *Electra*.) (3) The non-interference of the Chorus seems monstrous: yet in ancient times, when law was weak and punishment was chiefly the concern of the injured persons, and of no one else, the reluctance of bystanders to interfere was much greater than it is now in an ordered society.   Some oriental countries, and perhaps even California or Texas, could afford us some startling instances of impassiveness among bystanders.

P. 12, l. 167, Oh, wild words!]—The Nurse breaks in, hoping to drown her mistress's dangerous self-betrayal.   Medea's murder of her brother (see Introduction, p. vi) was by ordinary standards her worst act, and seems not to have been known in Corinth.   It forms the climax of Jason's denunciation, l. 1334, p. 74.

P. 13, l. 190, Alas, the bold blithe bards, &c.]— Who is the speaker? According to the MSS. the Nurse, and there is some difficulty in taking the lines from her.   Yet (1) she has no reason to sing a song outside after saying that she is going in; and (2) it is quite necessary that she should take a little time indoors persuading Medea to come out.   The words seems to suit the lips of an impersonal Chorus.

The general sense of the poem is interesting.   It is

an apology for tragedy. It gives the tragic poet's conception of the place of his art in the service of humanity, as against the usual feeling of the public, whose serious work is devoted to something else, and who " go to a play to be amused."

P. 14, l. 214, Women of Corinth, I am come, &c.] —These opening lines are a well-known *crux inter-pretum.* It is interesting to note, (1) that the Roman poet Ennius (ca. 200 B.C.) who translated the *Medea,* did not understand them in the least; while, on the other hand, the earliest Greek commentators seem not to have noticed that there was any difficulty in them worth commenting upon. That implies that while the acting tradition was alive and unbroken, the lines were easily understood; but when once the tradition failed, the meaning was lost. (The first commentator who deals with the passage is Irenæus, a scholar of the Augustan time.)

P. 15, l. 231, A herb most bruised is woman.]— This fine statement of the wrongs of women in Athens doubtless contains a great deal of the poet's own mind; but from the dramatic point of view it is justified in several ways. (1) Medea is seeking for a common ground on which to appeal to the Corinthian women. (2) She herself is now in the position of all others in which a woman is most hardly treated as compared with a man. (3) Besides this, one can see that, being a person of great powers and vehement will, she feels keenly her lack of outlet. If she had men's work to do, she could be a hero: debarred from proper action (from τὸ πράσσειν, *Hip.* 1019) she is bound to make mischief. Cf. p. 24, ll. 408, 409. " Things most vain, &c."

There is a slight anachronism in applying the Attic system of dowries to primitive times. Medea's contemporaries either lived in a "matriarchal" system without any marriage, or else were bought by their husbands for so many cows.

P. 17, l. 271, CREON.]—Observe the somewhat archaic abruptness of this scene, a sign of the early date of the play.

P. 18, l. 295, Wise beyond men's wont.]—Medea was a "wise woman," which in her time meant much the same as a witch or enchantress. She did really know more than other women; but most of this extra knowledge consisted—or was supposed to consist—either in lore of poisons and charms, or in useless learning and speculation.

P. 18, l. 304, A seed of strife, an Eastern dreamer, &c.]—The meaning of these various "ill names" is not certain. Cf. l. 808, p. 46. Most scholars take θατέρου τρόπου ("of the other sort") to mean "the opposite of a dreamer."

P. 20, ll. 333-4, What would I with thy pains?]—A conceit almost in the Elizabethan style, as if by taking "pains" away from Creon, she would have them herself.

P. 20, l. 335, Not that! Not that!]—Observe what a dislike Medea has of being touched: cf. l. 370 ("my flesh been never stained," &c.) and l. 496 ("poor, poor right hand of mine!"), pp. 22 and 28.

P. 22, l. 364, Defeat on every side.]—Observe (1) that in this speech Medea's vengeance is to take the form of a clear fight to the death against the three guilty persons. It is both courageous and,

G

judged by the appropriate standard, just. (2) She wants to save her own life, not from cowardice, but simply to make her revenge more complete. To kill her enemies and escape is victory. To kill them and die with them is only a drawn battle. Other enemies will live and "laugh." (3) Already in this first soliloquy there is a suggestion of that strain of madness which becomes unmistakable later on in the play. ("Oh, I have tried so many thoughts of murder," &c., and especially the lashing of her own fury, " Awake thee now, Medea.")

P. 24, l. 405, Thief's daughter: lit. "a child of Sisyphus."]—Sisyphus, an ancient king of Corinth, was one of the well-known sinners punished in Tartarus. Medea's father, Aiêtês, was a brother of Circe, and born of the Sun.

P. 24, l. 409, Things most vain for help.]—See on ll. 230 ff.

P. 24, ll. 410–430, CHORUS.]—The song celebrates the coming triumph of Woman in her rebellion against Man; not by any means Woman as typifying the domestic virtues, but rather as the downtrodden, uncivilised, unreasoning, and fiercely emotional half of humanity. A woman who in defence of her honour and her rights will die sword in hand, slaying the man who wronged her, seems to the Chorus like a deliverer of the whole sex.

P. 24, l. 421, Old bards.]—Early literature in most countries contains a good deal of heavy satire on women: e.g. Hesiod's " Who trusts a woman trusts a thief; " or Phocylides' " Two days of a woman are very sweet: when you marry her and when you carry her to her grave."

It is curious how the four main Choruses of the *Medea* are divided each into two parts, distinct in subject and in metre.

P. 25, l. 439, Faith is no more sweet.]—Copied from a beautiful passage in Hesiod, *Works and Days*, 198 ff.: "There shall be no more sweetness found in the faithful man nor the righteous. . . . And at last up to Olympus from the wide-wayed earth, shrouding with white raiment their beautiful faces, go Ruth and Rebuking." (Aidos and Nemesis: *i.e.* the Ruth or Shame that you feel with reference to your own actions, and the Indignation or Disapproval that others feel.)

P. 27, ll. 478 ff., Bulls of fiery breath.]—Among the tasks set him by Aiêtês, Jason had to yoke two fire-breathing bulls, and plough with them a certain Field of Ares, sow the field with Dragon's teeth, and reap a harvest of earth-born or giant warriors which sprang from the seed. When all this was done, there remained the ancient serpent coiled round the tree where the Golden Fleece was hanging.

P. 29, l. 507, The first friends who sheltered me.]— *i.e.* the kindred of Pelias.

P. 29, l. 509, Blest of many a maid in Hellas.]— Jason was, of course, the great romantic hero of his time. Cf. his own words, l. 1340, p. 74.

Pp. 29 ff., ll. 523–575.—Jason's defence is made the weaker by his reluctance to be definitely insulting to Medea. He dares not say: "You think that, because you conceived a violent passion for me,—to which, I admit, I partly responded—I must live with you always; but the truth is, you are a savage with whom a civilised man cannot go on living." This point comes out unveiled in his later speech, l. 1329 ff., p. 74.

P. 30, ll. 536 ff., Our ordered life and justice.]—Jason has brought the benefits of civilisation to Medea! He is doubtless sincere, but the peculiar ironic cruelty of the plea is obvious.

P. 30, ll. 541 ff., The story of Great Medea, &c. . . . Unless our deeds have glory.]—This, I think, is absolutely sincere. To Jason ambition is everything. And, as Medea has largely shared his great deeds with him, he thinks that she cannot but feel the same. It seems to him contemptible that her mere craving for personal love should outweigh all the possible glories of life.

P. 31, l. 565, What more need hast thou of children?]—He only means, " of more children than you now have." But the words suggest to Medea a different meaning, and sow in her mind the first seed of the child-murder. See on the Aegeus scene below.

P. 34, l. 608, A living curse.]—Though she spoke no word, the existence of a being so deeply wronged would be a curse on her oppressors. So a murdered man's blood, or an involuntary cry of pain (Aesch. *Ag.* 237) on the part of an injured person is in itself fraught with a curse.

P. 35, ll. 627–641, CHORUS. Alas, the Love, &c.] —A highly characteristic Euripidean poem, keenly observant of fact, yet with a lyrical note penetrating all its realism. A love which really produces " good to man and glory," is treated in the next chorus, l. 844 ff., p. 49.

Pp. 37 ff., ll. 663–759, AEGEUS.]—This scene is generally considered to be a mere blot on the play, not, I think, justly. It is argued that the obvious purpose which the scene serves, the provision of an asylum for Medea, has no keen dramatic interest. The spectator would just as soon, or sooner, have her die. And, besides, her actual mode of escape is largely independent of Aegeus. Further, the arrival of Aegeus at this moment seems to be a mere coincidence (*Ar. Poetics*, 61 b, 23), and one cannot help suspecting that the Athenian poet was influenced by mere local interests in dragging in the Athenian king and the praises of Athens where they were not specially appropriate.

To these criticisms one may make some answer. (1) As to the coincidence, it is important to remember always that Greek tragedies are primarily historical plays, not works of fiction. They are based on definite *Logoi* or traditions (*Frogs*, l. 1052, p. 254) and therefore can, and should, represent accidental coincidences when it was a datum of the tradition that these coincidences actually happened. By Aristotle's time the practice had changed. The tragedies of his age were essentially fiction; and he tends to criticise the ancient tragedies by fictional standards.

Now it was certainly a datum in the Medea legend that she took refuge with Aegeus, King of Athens, and was afterwards an enemy to his son Theseus; but I think we may go further. This play pretty certainly has for its foundation the rites performed by the Corinthians at the Grave of the Children of Medea in the precinct of Hera Acraia near Corinth. See on l. 1379, p. 77. The legend in such cases is usually invented to explain the ritual; and I suspect that in the ritual, and, consequently, in the legend, there were two other data: first, a pursuit of Medea and her flight on a dragon-chariot, and, secondly, a meeting between Medea and Aegeus. (Both subjects are frequent on vase paintings, and may well be derived from historical pictures in some temple at Corinth.)

Thus, the meeting with Aegeus is probably not the free invention of Euripides, but one of the data supplied to him by his subject. But he has made it serve, as von Arnim was the first to perceive, a remarkable dramatic purpose. Aegeus was under a curse of childlessness, and his desolate condition suggests to Medea the ultimate form of her vengeance. She will make Jason childless. Cf. l. 670, " Children! Ah God, art childless? " (A childless king in antiquity was a miserable object: likely to be deposed and dishonoured, and to miss his due worship after death. See the fragments of Euripides' *Oineus*.)

There is also a further purpose in the scene, of a curious and characteristic kind. In several plays of Euripides, when a heroine hesitates on the verge of a crime, the thing that drives her over the brink is some sudden and violent lowering of her self-respect. Thus Phædra writes her false letter immediately after her public shame. Creûsa in the *Ion* turns murderous only after crying in the god's ears the story of her seduction. Medea, a princess and, as we have seen, a woman of rather proud chastity, feels, after the offer which she makes to Aegeus in this scene (l. 716 ff., p. 42), that she need shrink from nothing.

P. 38, l. 681, The hearth-stone of my sires of yore.]
—This sounds as if it meant Aegeus' own house: in reality, by an oracular riddle, it meant the house of

Pittheus, by whose daughter, Aethra, Aegeus became the father of Theseus.

P. 43, l. 731, An oath wherein to trust.]—Observe that Medea is deceiving Aegeus. She intends to commit a murder before going to him, and therefore wishes to bind him down so firmly that, however much he wish to repudiate her, he shall be unable. Hence this insistence on the oath and the exact form of the oath. (At this time, apparently, she scarcely thinks of the children, only of her revenge.)

P. 46, l. 808, No eastern dreamer, &c.]—See on l. 304.

P. 47, l. 820, The NURSE comes out.]—There is no indication in the original to show who comes out. But it is certainly a woman; as certainly it is not one of the Chorus; and Medea's words suit the Nurse well. It is an almost devilish act to send the Nurse, who would have died rather than take such a message had she understood it.

P. 48, ll. 824–846, The sons of Erechtheus, &c.]— This poem is interesting as showing the ideal conception of Athens entertained by a fifth-century Athenian. One might compare with it Pericles' famous speech in Thucydides, ii, where the emphasis is laid on Athenian "plain living and high thinking" and the freedom of daily life. Or, again, the speeches of Aethra in Euripides' *Suppliant Women*, where more stress is laid on mercy and championship of the oppressed.

The allegory of " Harmony," as a sort of Korê, or Earth-maiden, planted by all the Muses in the soil of Attica, seems to be an invention of the poet. Not any given Art or Muse, but a spirit which unites and harmonises all, is the special spirit of Athens. The Attic connection with Erôs, on the other hand, is old and traditional. But Euripides has transformed the primitive nature-god into a mystic and passionate longing for " all manner of high deed," a Love which, different from that described in the preceding chorus, really ennobles human life.

This first part of the Chorus is, of course, suggested by Aegeus; the second is more closely connected with the action of the play. " How can Medea dream of asking that stainless land to shelter her crimes? But the whole plan of her revenge is not only wicked but impossible. She simply could not do such a thing, if she tried."

Pp. 50 ff., l. 869, The second scene with Jason.]— Dicæarchus, and perhaps his master Aristotle also, seems to have complained of Medea's bursting into tears in this scene, instead of acting her part consistently—a very prejudiced criticism. What strikes one about Medea's assumed rôle is that in it she remains so like herself and so unlike another woman. Had she really determined to yield to Jason, she would have done so in just this way, keen-sighted and yet passionate. One is reminded of the deceits of half-insane persons, which are due not so much to conscious art as to the emergence of another side of the personality.

P. 54, l. 949, Fine robings, &c.]—Repeated from l. 786, p. 46, where it came full in the midst of Medea's avowal of her murderous purpose. It startles one here, almost as though she had spoken out the word " murder " in some way which Jason could not understand.

P. 56, l. 976, CHORUS.]—The inaction of the
Chorus women during the last scene will not bear
thinking about, if we regard them as real human
beings, like, for instance, the Bacchæ and the Trojan
Women in the plays that bear their name. Still
there is not only beauty, but, I think, great dramatic
value in the conventional and almost mystical quality
of this Chorus, and also in the low and quiet tone of
that which follows, l. 1081 ff.

P. 59, ll. 1021 ff., Why does Medea kill her
children?]—She acts not for one clearly stated reason,
like a heroine in Sardou, but for many reasons, both
conscious and subconscious, as people do in real
life. Any analysis professing to be exact would
be misleading, but one may note some elements
in her feeling: (1) She had played dangerously long
with the notion of making Jason childless. (2) When
she repented of this (l. 1046, p. 60) the children
had already been made the unconscious murderers
of the princess. They were certain to be slain, perhaps with tortures, by the royal kindred. (3) Medea
might take them with her to Athens and trust to
the hope of Aegeus' being able and willing to protect
them. But it was a doubtful chance, and she would
certainly be in a position of weakness and inferiority
if she had the children to protect. (4) In the midst
of her passionate half-animal love for the children,
there was also an element of hatred, because they
were Jason's: cf. l. 112, p. 8. (5) She also seems
to feel, in a sort of wild-beast way, that by killing them
she makes them more her own: cf. l. 793, p. 46,
" Mine, whom no hand shall steal from me away; "
l. 1241, p. 68, " touched of none beside." (6) Euri-

pides had apparently observed how common it is, when a woman's mind is deranged by suffering, that her madness takes the form of child-murder. The terrible lines in which Medea speaks to the " Wrath " within her, as if it were a separate being (l. 1056, p. 60), seem to bear out this view.

P. 59, l. 1038, Other shapes of life.]—A mystical conception of death. Cf. *Ion*, 1067, where almost exactly the same phrase is used.

P. 61, l. 1078, I know to what bad deeds, &c.]— This expression of double consciousness was immensely famous in antiquity. It is quoted by Lucian, Plutarch, Clement, Galen, Synesius, Hierocles, Arrian, Simplicius, besides being imitated, *e.g.* by Ovid: " video meliora proboque, Deteriora sequor."

P. 63, l. 1123 ff., MESSENGER.]—A pendant to the Attendant's entrance above, l. 1002. The Attendant, bringing apparently good news, is received with a moan of despair, the Messenger of calamity with serene satisfaction. Cf. the Messenger who announces the death of Pentheus in the *Bacchæ*.

P. 65, l. 1162, Dead self.]—The reflection in the glass, often regarded as ominous or uncanny in some way.

P. 66, l. 1176, The cry turned strangely to its opposite.]—The notion was that an evil spirit could be scared away by loud cheerful shouts—*ololugæ*. But while this old woman is making an *ololugê*, she sees that the trouble is graver than she thought, and the cheerful cry turns into a wail.

P. 68, l. 1236, Women, my mind is clear.]— With the silence in which Medea passes over the success of her vengeance compare Theseus' words, *Hip.*,

l. 1260, " I laugh not, neither weep, at this fell doom."

P. 69, l. 1249, Thou shalt weep hereafter.]—Cf. *Othello*, v. ii., " Be thus when thou art dead, and I will kiss thee, And love thee after."

P. 69, ll. 1251 ff.—This curious prayer to the Sun to " save " Medea—both from the crime of killing her children and the misfortune of being caught by her enemies—is apparently meant to prepare us for the scene of the Dragon Chariot. Notice the emphasis laid on the divine origin of Medea's race and her transformation to " a voice of Hell."

P. 71, ll. 1278 ff., Death of the children.]—The door is evidently barred, since Jason has to use crow-bars to open it in l. 1317. Cf. the end of Maeterlinck's *Mort de Tintagiles*.

P. 71, l. 1281, A mother slew her babes in days of yore, &c.]—Ino, wife of Athamas, King of Thebes, nursed the infant Dionysus. For this Hera punished her with madness. She killed her two children, Learchus and Melicertes, and leaped into the sea. (There are various versions of the story.)—Observe the technique: just as the strain is becoming intoler-able, we are turned away from tragedy to pure poetry. See on *Hip.* 731.

P. 74, l. 1320, This, that shall save me from mine enemies' rage.]—There is nothing in the words of the play to show what " this " is, but the Scholiast explains it as a chariot drawn by winged serpents, and the stage tradition seems to be clear on the subject. See note to the Aegeus scene (p. 88).

This first appearance of Medea " above, on the

tower " (Scholiast) seems to me highly effective. The result is to make Medea into something like a *dea ex machinâ*, who prophesies and pronounces judgment. See Introduction.

P. 76, l. 1370, They are dead, they are dead!]— This wrangle, though rather like some scenes in Norse sagas, is strangely discordant for a Greek play. It seems as if Euripides had deliberately departed from his usual soft and reflective style of ending in order to express the peculiar note of discord which is produced by the so-called " satisfaction " of revenge. Medea's curious cry: " Oh, thy voice! It hurts me sore! " shows that the effect is intentional.

P. 77, l. 1379, A still green sepulchre.]—There was a yearly festival in the precinct of Hera Acraia, near Corinth, celebrating the deaths of Medea's children. This festival, together with its ritual and " sacred legend," evidently forms the germ of the whole tragedy. Cf. the Trozenian rites over the tomb of Hippolytus, *Hip.* 1424 ff.

P. 77, l. 1386, The hands of thine old Argo.]— Jason, left friendless and avoided by his kind, went back to live with his old ship, now rotting on the shore. While he was sleeping under it, a beam of wood fell upon him and broke his head. It is a most grave mistake to treat the line as spurious.

GEORGE ALLEN & UNWIN LTD

London: 40 Museum Street, W.C.1

Auckland: 24 Wyndham Street
Bombay: 15 Graham Road, Ballard Estate, Bombay 1
Bridgetown: P.O. Box 222
Buenos Aires: Escritorio 454–459, Florida 165
Calcutta: 17 Chittarajan Avenue, Calcutta 13
Cape Town: 68 Shortmarket Street
Hong Kong: 44 Mody Road, Kowloon
Ibadan: P.O. Box 62
Karachi: Karachi Chambers, McLeod Road
Madras: Mohan Mansions, 38c Mount Road, Madras 6
Mexico: Villalongin 32–10, Piso, Mexico 5, D.F.
Nairobi: P.O. Box 4536
New Delhi: 13–14 Asaf Ali Road, New Delhi 1
Ontario: 81 Curlew Drive, Don Mills
Philippines: 7 Waling-Waling Street, Roxas District,
Quezon City
Sao Paulo: Caixa Postal 8675
Singapore: 36c Prinsep Street, Singapore 7
Sydney: N.S.W.: Bradbury House, 55 York Street
Tokyo: 10 Kanda-Ogawamachi, 3-Chome, Chiyoda-Ku

THE COMPLETE PLAYS
OF ÆSCHYLUS

TRANSLATED INTO
ENGLISH RHYMING VERSE WITH
COMMENTARIES AND NOTES BY

GILBERT MURRAY

Cr. 8vo. 18s. net

An Omnibus Volume of:

THE SUPPLIANT WOMEN

'Impossible to ask for more grace of accomplishment.'
Manchester Guardian

THE PERSIANS

'Shows his usual felicity in varying the choral metres to suit the changing rhythms of the Greek and in finding English to fit the heights and depths of Æschylean phraseology.' *Manchester Guardian*

THE SEVEN AGAINST THEBES

'Skilful, vigorous and inspiring.' *Quarterly Review*

PROMETHEUS BOUND

THE AGAMEMNON

'A success beyond what seemed possible and conveys in his English the intense horror and passion of the Greek.'
Sunday Times

THE CHOËPHOROE

THE EUMENIDES

'In some ways his most notable achievement. . . . A noble version.' *The Observer*

COLLECTED PLAYS
OF EURIPIDES

TRANSLATED INTO
ENGLISH RHYMING VERSE WITH
COMMENTARIES AND NOTES BY

GILBERT MURRAY

Cr. 8vo. 21s. net

An Omnibus Volume of:

ALCESTIS, MEDEA, HIPPOLYTUS, ELECTRA,
THE TROJAN WOMEN, IPHIGENIA IN TAURIS,
THE BACCHAE, RHESUS

★

ŒDIPUS AT COLONUS: Sophocles

Translated into English rhyming verse with Introduction
and Notes by GILBERT MURRAY   Cr. 8vo. 5s. net

'Nothing can destroy or even dim Professor Murray's great
contribution to our literature in enriching it with the first modern
renderings of these classics of Ancient Greece. The pathos and the
terror he evokes in this version of the Colonus, and the exquisite
music of the interspersed Choruses, make it a worthy addition to
his translations of *Œdipus Rex* and the *Antigone*; the two plays
with which, without forming a trilogy, it is closely linked.'
New English Weekly

'In Dr. Murray the gifted scholarship, the penetrative human
insight and the mastery of the rhyming couplet are still vigorously
united to impart to his latest work the quality which has made his
translations of Greek plays so notable a contribution to the cause of
the humanities in our time . . . it is hard to think that any of Dr.
Murray's translations can have been more pleasing or felicitous than
this.' *The Times Literary Supplement.*

By J. A. K. THOMSON

SHAKESPEARE AND THE CLASSICS

by J. A. K. Thomson

Large Cr. 8vo.   18s. net

There has been of late a revival of interest in the extent of Shakespeare's indebtedness to the ancient classics. As the question is one on which a classical scholar may fairly be expected to offer an opinion, it has been re-examined by Professor J. A. K. Thomson. His study has led him to make two suggestions. The first is that the belief held about Shakespeare by his intimates that he had not a scholarly acquaintance with Latin or Greek has not been seriously shaken. The second is that the tragic conception underlying Plutarch's *Life of Julius Cæsar* was completely grasped by Shakespeare, who was thereby enabled to create a new kind of drama—Shakespearian tragedy—which, owing nothing to the letter, owes a great deal to the spirit, of Greek Tragedy.

Serious students of English literature have long felt the want of a book which should define the extent and character of the influence which has been exerted upon it throughout its history by the ancient classics. To supply this want is the main purpose of *The Classical Background of English Literature*.

It is not expected of the reader that he should himself be able to read Latin or Greek. But, as the writer deals with the relations between ancient and modern literature, it is hoped that the book may have some interest and value for classical as well as English students. Neither is there anything in it to deter the general reader who is fond of literature for its own sake.

'A wise and stimulating book which can be strongly recommended to all students of English literature whether they have had a classical education or not.' *Education.*

GILBERT MURRAY

'Gilbert Murray's translations . . . are still by any standards remarkably skilful . . . he shirks no difficulties and really knows what the Greek words mean.' SIR MAURICE BOWRA

'Gilbert Murray's . . . were epoch-making, there had been many translations before him, but his were the first that enabled ordinary educated people who did not know Greek to enjoy and appreciate the masterpieces of Greek drama, and especially of Euripides. For the first time the public realized that these were great poetry and great plays. Poetry, if it is to live in another language, must be translated by a poet, and Murray was that as well as a great scholar. One witness to his success is the amazing circulation of his translations and the way in which they began to be widely acted . . . I do not believe that they will be replaced in popular favour or lose their value.

Murray lectured on the plays in the original and anyone who was fortunate enough to hear these lectures is not likely to forget his superb interpretations. Something of these survive in the introductions and notes appended to the translations, which add greatly to their value.'

SIR RICHARD LIVINGSTONE

The Translations of Greek Plays

AESCHYLUS

The Agamemnon; The Choë-phoroe; The Eumenides; The Suppliant Women, Prometheus Bound; The Seven Against Thebes; The Persians.

EURIPIDES

Alcestis; Electra; Hippoly-tus; Iphigenia in Tauris; Medea; Rhesus; The Bacchae; The Trojan Women; Ion.

ARISTOPHANES

The Frogs; The Birds; The Knights.

MENANDER

The Arbitration; The Rape of the Locks.

SOPHOCLES

The Antigone; Oedipus, King of Thebes; Oedipus at Colonus; The Wife of Heracles.

THE ORESTEIA

Revised 2nd Edition, Cloth 21s net. Paper 12s 6d

THE COMPLETE PLAYS OF AESCHYLUS

18s net

Printed in Great Britain
by Amazon